ALL KIDS
scrapbook pages

EVERY CHILD IS A **SUCCESS** STORY WAITING TO BEGIN

the growing up years

MEMORY
MAKERS
BOOKS

MANAGING EDITOR MaryJo Regier

EDITOR Amy Glander

ART DIRECTOR Nick Nyffeler

GRAPHIC DESIGNERS Jordan Kinney, Robin Rozum

ART ACQUISITIONS EDITOR Janetta Abucejo Wieneke

CRAFT EDITOR Jodi Amidei

PHOTOGRAPHER Ken Trujillo

CONTRIBUTING PHOTOGRAPHERS Jennifer Reeves

ART CAPTION WRITERS Elizabeth Shaffer Harlan, Heather Marie Wells

EDITORIAL SUPPORT Karen Cain, Emily Curry Hitchingham, Lydia Rueger, Dena Twinem

CONTRIBUTING MEMORY MAKERS MASTERS Jessie Baldwin, Jenn Brookover, Christine Brown, Sheila

Doherty, Angie Head, Jeniece Higgins, Nicola Howard, Kelli Noto, Torrey Scott,

Shannon Taylor, Denise Tucker

Memory Makers® All Kids Scrapbook Pages

Published by Memory Makers Books, an imprint of F+W Publications, Inc.
12365 Huron Street, Suite 500, Denver, CO 80234
Phone (800) 254-9124
First edition. Printed in the United States.
09 08 07 06 05 5 4 3 2 1

Library of Congress Cataloging-in-Publication Data

All kids scrapbook pages : the growing up years.
      p. cm.
   Includes index.
   ISBN 1-892127-63-6
   1. Photograph albums. 2. Photographs--Conservation and Restoration. 3. Scrapbooks. 4.
Children--Portraits. I. Memory Makers Books.

TR465.A457 2005
745.593--dc22

                                                                                    2005047897

Distributed to trade and art markets by
F+W Publications, Inc.
4700 East Galbraith Road, Cincinnati, OH 45236
Phone (800) 289-0963
ISBN 1-892127-63-6

Distributed in Canada by Fraser Direct
100 Armstrong Avenue
Georgetown, ON, Canada L7G 5S4
Tel: (905) 877-4411

Distributed in the U.K. and Europe by David & Charles
Brunel House, Newton Abbot, Devon, TQ12 4PU, England
Tel: (+44) 1626 323200, Fax: (+44) 1626 323319
E-mail: mail@davidandcharles.co.uk

Distributed in Australia by Capricorn Link
P.O. Box 704, S. Windsor NSW, 2756 Australia
Tel: (02) 4577-3555

Memory Makers Books is the home of *Memory Makers*, the scrapbook magazine dedicated to educating and inspiring scrapbookers.
To subscribe, or for more information, call (800) 366-6465.
Visit us on the Internet at www.memorymakersmagazine.com.

Kids

This book belongs to

_____

We dedicate this book to all of our contributors who graciously shared their spectacular kid scrapbook pages with us and who may now be even more inspired to preserve cherished childhood memories.

TABLE OF CONTENTS

CHAPTER ONE 8-31

LIVE

43 eye-catching page ideas that capture kids in motion. Everything from taking a cool dip at the beach to climbing trees, playing sports and hanging out with friends.

49 endearing page ideas that celebrate that crazy little thing called love. Covering everything from favorite things to love for pets, siblings and cousins, these pages are sure to melt your heart.

LOVE

CHAPTER TWO 32-57

LAUGH CHAPTER THREE 58-79

40 picture-perfect pages that show giddy boys and girls at their silliest—from soft giggles to laugh-out-loud chuckles, these spunky kids are all smiles!

49 innovative page ideas devoted to the art of discovery—from playing musical instruments and reading favorite books to exploring nature and earning scouting badges.

CHAPTER FOUR 80-107 LEARN

Just what is it about kids that can set our adrenaline soaring, make our hearts melt, put us into fits of laughter and get our minds pondering the unique wisdom of children? Being a kid is a curious blend of energy and enthusiasm, discovery and determination, giggles and grins, but most of all—joy!

Childhood is full of good times, and ones you'll want to remember in scrapbooks. I fondly remember the preschool days of my own childhood—coloring with crayons, singing songs, learning the alphabet. Then the next phase of birthday parties, sleepovers, swimming at the beach, sledding and making snow angels. At last I reached the rite of passage when my parents finally allowed me to go to summer camp. With this stage came class field trips to Discovery World Museum and The Shedd Aquarium, earning scouting badges and participating in sports.

All Kids Scrapbook Pages features over 150 captivating layouts all about kids—what they do, what they learn, what they love and what makes them laugh. This book is intended to help you capture the precious moments and milestones of your one-of-a-kind kid. You'll find eye-catching pages that will inspire you to document your youngster in motion. But start now while he or she is still a young whippersnapper mesmerized at each new experience.

With this book, I hope you will be inspired to preserve all of your child's animated, lovable, amusing and proud moments based on the ideas inside. So celebrate the life and times of your child through scrapbook pages that capture the essence of childhood and all its zany moments.

Amy

Amy Glander, Associate Editor

HOW TO MAKE A SCRAPBOOK PAGE
Building a page from the background out

Start with a selection of photos for a single page and gather any appropriate memorabilia. Select a background paper that pulls one color from your photos or establishes the mood you wish to convey. You may wish to choose additional papers that complement your theme or photos. Pick out or make page additions that complement photos if desired. Loosely assemble photos, title, journaling, memorabilia and page accents to form a visually appealing layout. Trim and mat photos, then mount in place with adhesive. Add title and journaling. Complete the page with any additional accents. For instructions on how to replicate this page exactly, see page 109.

SUPPLIES FOR MAKING LASTING ALBUMS

The use of high-quality scrapbook materials will ensure your cherished childhood memories stay the course of time.

We recommend the following:

- Archival-quality albums

- PVC-free page protectors

- Acid- and lignin-free papers

- Acid-free and photo-safe adhesives

- Pigment-ink pens and markers

- PVC-free memorabilia keepers, sleeves or envelopes

- Flat, photo-safe embellishments
(encapsulate or place away from photos if questionable)

- De-acidifying spray for news clippings or documents

Kids are always on a quest for fun. They love imagining and pretending, naturally gravitate to out-door play and will be up for just about anything that involves spending time with friends. Some will spend carefree summer days climbing trees, running through the sprinkler or chasing butterflies. Some are explorers, always on an expedition searching for the X that marks the spot. Others prefer the competitive dynamism that sports and games offer. And what kid would turn down a trip to the local water park or city zoo? Childhood invites all kinds of good times for youngsters, so why not encourage their vivacious disposition with opportunities to live life to the absolute fullest? Whether they're dressing up like their favorite movie character, riding waves on a boogie board at the beach or blowing bubbles on the back porch, kids will never cease to captivate us with their zealous nature and imperishable energy. Rain or shine, kids will always answer life's call for adventure.

A GRASSY GANG

Shannon captured the action, grins and grime of this spontaneous day of fun in her bright layout. Trim vertical strips of yellow and striped papers to create background. Mount overlay transparency to left side of page. Crop photos. Add one to blue frame and mat others. Arrange on the spread. Use alcohol-based stamping ink to color acrylic tags. Add rub-on words and adhere to page. Connect jump rings and add to page elements. Print and cut out title font. Cover with liquid lacquer and dry. Mat on pink cardstock, trim close to letters and adhere. Print journaling on a transparency and add to layout. Embellish with ribbon and rub-ons.

Shannon Taylor, Bristol, Tennessee

Supplies: Patterned papers (Rusty Pickle); transparency (Creative Imaginations); acrylic tiles, rub-on letters and words, jump rings (Junkitz); faux leather frame (EK Success); alcohol-based inks (Ranger); dimensional adhesive (JudiKins); periwinkle, pink and mint green cardstocks; pink ribbon

POGO FUN

Polka dots create a feeling of fun and movement on this page about learning how to use a pogo stick. Affix brown polka-dot paper to blue cardstock. Attach photo. Affix letter stickers for title down the left side of the page. Fold rust cardstock to create card for hidden journaling. Mount photo on cover of card, and attach ribbon on inside for opening. Affix letter stickers for remainder of title below the first picture. Print journaling onto white cardstock, trim and adhere to inside of card. Use rub-ons for date in upper right corner.

Erin Sweeney, Twinsburg, Ohio

Supplies: Cardstock (Bazzill); brown patterned paper and letter stickers (American Crafts); rub-on letters (Autumn Leaves); ribbon (Darice)

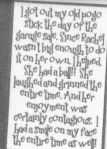

PUSH IT

Kitty created a gritty feeling for her layout by using etched letter accents. Tear patterned papers and adhere to black cardstock background. Mount photo on patterned paper and again on black cardstock; attach to page. Distress etched letter accents and fill in with metallic paints. Type journaling and print onto bronze cardstock. Cut and adhere to page. Cut out phrases from patterned paper and adhere to page. Frame title with patterned slide mount. Affix second photo at bottom of page.

Kitty Foster, Snellville, Georgia

Supplies: Patterned paper, etched letter accents, patterned slide mount (Deluxe Designs); metallic paint (Jacquard); cardstock (Bazzill)

BOYHOOD

Clean, simple lines and geometric paper accent the freshness of a boyhood day at the beach. Mat photo and patterned paper with black cardstock; adhere both to page. Adhere photo frames to front of folded black cardstock "mini cards." Adhere both to page. Journal inside photo mats with silver marker. Adhere fabric label to page and affix letter sticker in bottom right-hand corner.

Kimberly Kesti, Phoenix, Arizona

Supplies: Cardstock (Bazzill, Scrapworks); patterned paper (NRN Designs); photo frames (Memory Lane); letter sticker (American Crafts); fabric label (Me & My Big Ideas); pen

YOU ARE SUNSHINE

Martha used orange and green patterned paper to accentuate the colors of summer and sunshine. For left page, mat all photos on black cardstock and adhere to patterned paper background. Mount definition on black cardstock. Chalk with lime green and yellow and mount on page. Affix stickers to tag, add fibers and adhere to page. Print journaling onto transparency, cut and affix. For right page, cut large photo into sections. Mount three smaller photos on black cardstock. Adhere all photos to page. Affix text sticker below large picture, and in top center of page. Affix stickers to tags, add fiber and adhere to page. Mount definition on black cardstock and adhere to page. Thread orange fiber through letter charm and attach to page.

Martha Crowther, Salem, New Hampshire

Supplies: Patterned paper, tags (Scrappy Cat); fiber (Fibers By The Yard); word stickers (NRN Designs, Wordsworth); water stickers (Creative Imaginations); definitions (Making Memories); chalks

THE BEACH

Tracy used browns and cool blues to set the tone for a relaxing day at the beach. Adhere white speciality paper to left corner of brown cardstock background. Tear edges of patterned paper and crumple; attach to green cardstock. Write title on torn buff cardstock with dots in brown pen. Adhere to bronze shimmer cardstock and wrap entire element with fibers. Attach to right side of page. Crumple and tear buff cardstock. Distress with metallic rub-ons. Colorize and tear edges of smaller photo and mount onto blue cardstock. Adhere to larger piece of buff cardstock and connect to smaller pieces using twisted copper wire. Attach to page at top and bottom with copper brads. Triple mat larger photo and attach to page using foam squares.

Tracy Babineau, Truro, Nova Scotia, Canada

Supplies: Patterned paper (PSX Design); maruyama paper (Magenta); metallic rub-ons (Craf-T); copper wire; mini brads; fibers; photo twin photo tinting pens; buff, brown, green and bronze shimmer cardstocks

WE'VE GOT TICKETS TO RIDE

Shannon included an amazing 17 photos on this computer-generated spread consisting of bright, high-contrasting colors. To border the page, she used a close-up photo of one of the ride cars. Enlarge close-up photo of ride and place on left side of spread. Duplicate the image, crop it and place it on far right. Open a blue graphics box and position small cropped photos inside. Add focal photo on left. Frame box in deep red. Add the same frame to remaining cropped, sized photos and arrange on layouts. Type title, adding an inner shadow and glow. Enhance the letters by applying bevel and embossing commands. Create a text box that follows the curve on the ride photo and add journaling.

Shannon Taylor, Bristol, Tennessee

Supplies: Image-editing software (Adobe Photoshop)

SUN BABIES

Creating her own garden of punched flowers, Colleen designed a playful page featuring her sunny summer kids. Trim strips of pink, spring green and yellow cardstocks to frame three edges of purple paper. Add a green strip to right side of page. Trim random strips of colored paper resembling stems and adhere to purple background. Mat color photo onto pink paper. Create a larger mat with blue and yellow papers. Adhere black-and-white focal-point photo and matted color photo to background. Punch conchos, along with words, into the green cardstock strip. Add a layer of liquid lacquer to each concho and allow to dry. Create title blocks using stickers and die-cut word matted and embellished with square brads, clip, blue twine and a charm. Print journaling on cardstock, cut and mount. Add template-cut flowers across the page. Embellish flowers with brads and a small bit of twine for the centers. Add letter sticker names.

*Colleen Macdonald, Winthrop,
Washington, Australia*

Supplies: Patterned papers, coated linen thread, square paper clip, conchos and die-cut words (Scrapworks); letter stickers and flower-cutting template (Provo Craft); crystal lacquer (Ranger); laugh charm (Beads & Plenty More); square brads; spring green, pink, yellow and lavender cardstocks

IMAGINATION

Stripes and a variety of patterned papers give Kitty's page a feeling of movement and energy. Gently brush blue patterned paper and green paper with white paint. Adhere to page, positioning green sheet at an angle on top of blue sheet. Cut square frames out of maroon cardstock and striped paper. Overlap and adhere to page. Brush thin strip of maroon cardstock with white paint, and attach to page using brads. Affix stickers to spell title. Mat photos on blue cardstock. Adhere horizontal photo to painted maroon cardstock and attach both photos to page. Print journaling on blue cardstock, cut into square and drybrush with white paint. Once dry, attach to page using brads. Attach metal plaque to bottom left of page.

Kitty Foster, Snellville, Georgia

Supplies: *Patterned papers (Chatterbox); maroon cardstock (National Cardstock); metal plaque (Making Memories); alphabet stickers (Pebbles); blue brads; white paint*

SOAKED

Legoland held many surprises for Sheila and her family, including a water fountain to explore. Wavy strips of colorful patterned papers reminiscent of water reflect the fun and excitement the kids shared. Crop photos and cut wavy strips of patterned papers. Cut two thin strips of rainbow striped paper. Crop logo photo to fit label holder. Create journaling, title and date in image-editing software. Change colors of text to coordinate with patterned papers. Print and crop. Adhere elements to spread by layering wavy strips, journaling blocks, photos, mesh and rainbow strips. Secure label holder with brads. Embellish page with acrylic words, floss and ribbons.

Sheila Doherty, Coeur d'Alene, Idaho

Supplies: *Patterned papers (Carolee's Creations, KI Memories); vellum (KI Memories); circle cutter (Provo Craft); acrylic words (Doodlebug Design); metal label holder and embroidery floss (Making Memories); white mesh (Magic Mesh); image-editing software (Adobe Photoshop); ribbon (Morex Corporation); yellow cardstock*

The scrapbook layout contains the following text elements:

ANATOMY

A SQUARE GAME

#1 - Sit around & WAIT! Wait for the adults, wait for the kids...wait.

#2 - You need a certified "4-square engineer to design the square.

#3 - Setting the rules. This usually involves much heated debate but only minor physical violence.

#4 - The serve. If you don't have a good serve you won't keep the top spot for long.

#5 - One armed play. This option requires balance as well as skill. This is only for the advanced group.

#6 - Being quick & nimble is the way to keep in the game

#7- The "cheering section," can infuse the game with high energy. If you're a poor sport - expect to be BOO'ed.

#8- Strategy and alliances is as important as quickness & agility. If three are gunning for one, the one is bound to get knocked out sooner or later.

Children & adults alike love a good game of 4-square. Whether you're competitive or just want to have some fun with your neighbors, there's room for you in the game.

ANATOMY OF A FOUR-SQUARE GAME

Sande brings a traditional neighborhood four-square game to life in this vivid two-page layout. For left page, adhere patterned paper and photos to page. Sew strips of stiped patterned paper between photos. Attach chipboard letters to top of page. Tie fibers onto patterned paper, mount plastic number and adhere to page. Tie fibers to tag stickers and affix to page. Cut two circles from patterned paper and adhere behind two wooden letters. Add stamped images and words and rub-on letters. For right page, adhere photos and journaling printed on cardstock to page. Divide sections with strips of overlapped patterned paper affixed to page. Add rub-on numerals to photos.

Sande Krieger, Salt Lake City, Utah

Supplies: *Blue cardstock (Bazzill); patterned paper (Scenic Route Paper Co.); chipboard letters and wooden words (Li'l Davis Designs); number 4, hand stamp (Making Memories); ribbons (May Arts); rub-on letters (Autumn Leaves); tag stickers (Doodlebug Design); word stamp (EK Success); distress ink (Ranger); brown cardstock*

QUEST FOR FUN

Metal washers and silver mesh add a masculine feel to Jenn's layout. Trim blocks of patterned paper and blue cardstock. Using acrylic paint, stamp title and numerals on patterned paper. Print journaling on transparency and trim. Layer blocks and transparency and adhere to background. Crop focal-point photo and paint around edges. Cut strip of black cardstock and adhere over transparency. Add photos to layout. Using circle punch, punch five circles from black cardstock. Paint one washer red with acrylic paint. Use circles to mat five washers. Add additional washers to strip of black cardstock. Stamp remainder of title with black stamping ink.

Jenn Brookover, San Antonio, Texas

Supplies: Patterned paper (Daisy D's, Far and Away); foam stamps (Making Memories); mesh (K&S Metals); circle punch (All Night Media); transparency; black stamping ink; acrylic paint; washers; black pen

FUN & GAMES

Images of a traditional board game are used to create this vivid page about playing board games. Cut "cards" from patterned paper and attach to top of page. Affix letter stickers to cards to create title. Adhere patterned paper to cardstock. Adhere pink cardstock on top of patterned paper. Mount photos on blue and green cardstock and attach to page. Attach large metal alphabets to page using silver brads. Attach small metal alphabets using glue dots. Adhere black cardstock on top of patterned paper. Print journaling onto white cardstock and mount on black cardstock. Use label maker to create title for journaling block and affix to page. Attach black train to bottom of journaling.

Tricia Rubens, Castle Rock, Colorado

Supplies: Patterned paper and cardstock (Bazzill, EK Success); letter stickers (Doodlebug Design); metal alphabets (Making Memories); label maker (Dymo); silver brads

MEMORIES

Using earthy tones, Colleen created this page of her sons' bowling expedition. Cut blocks of initials patterned paper and layer with photos onto patterned paper background. Wrap mounted photos with ribbon, tie knot and adhere to page. Add printed tag, border stickers and journaling block printed on transparency. Thread twine through hand-printed tags and use a safety pin to attach them to ribbon.

Colleen Stearns,
Natrona Heights, Pennsylvania

Supplies: Patterned papers (Basic Grey, Deluxe Designs); tag and border stickers (Pebbles); ribbon (May Arts); decorative brads (Making Memories); metal-rimmed tags (Rusty Pickle); distress ink (Ranger); transparency; safety pin; twine; black pen

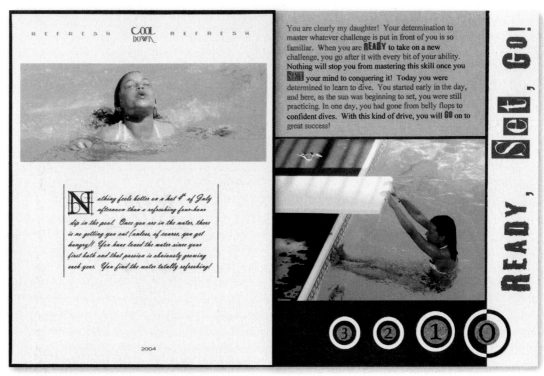

REFRESH

Using a graphic-style design, Sue created this page of her daughter taking a refreshing dip in the pool. For left page, stamp watermark using blue ink and floral foam stamp onto white cardstock. Print title and journaling using Internet fonts in black ink. Adhere photo under title and affix cardstock to black background. For right page, print and stamp journaling on light brown cardstock, cut to size and adhere over dark brown cardstock background. Stamp title on white cardstock, cut into a strip and adhere down right side of page. Adhere focal-point photo. Adhere number stickers to cork circles and adhere to page. Use circle punch to cut circles from white and brown cardstocks; adhere around cork circles.

Sue Thomas, Anoka, Minnesota

Supplies: Cardstock (Bazzill); foam floral stamp (Making Memories); chalk ink (Clearsnap); watermark ink (Tsukineko)

...WITH ABANDON

Dawn combined patterned papers and distress ink to accentuate boyhood abandon. Mat large photo on blue cardstock. Adhere to green patterned page. Attach strip of striped paper next to photo. Adhere blue patterned rectangle to lower right side of page. Attach dotted strip of paper. Print title onto patterned paper and cut out with craft knife; adhere vertically on lower right of page. Repeat process for remainder of title. Affix letter sticker at the beginning of word. Print definition onto vellum and trim. Cut out a half circle to create a pocket and attach to page with brads. Print journaling onto blue cardstock. Affix polka-dot strip and pull-tab to edge with staple. Attach two smaller photos. Distress action stickers with black ink and affix randomly throughout page. Print photo onto small piece of canvas, fray edges and fasten to word sticker with small safety pin. Distress tag and write date. Tie on key charm and attach to strip of polka-dot paper. Attach small blue frame and bottle cap.

Dawn Burden, Franklin, Tennessee

Supplies: Patterned paper, cardstock (KI Memories, Li'l Davis Designs); stickers (Creative Imaginations); colored staples (Making Memories); safety pin, bottle cap (Li'l Davis Designs); brads (Jo-Ann Stores); mini frame (KI Memories); key charm (Manto Fev); inkjet canvas (Fredrix); black marker; black ink; vellum

BOYS WILL BE BOYS

Blue patterned paper gives Gemiel's page an all-boy feeling. Trim large block of light blue cardstock and adhere over dark blue background. Trim large block of patterned paper and adhere to left side of layout. Weave ribbons through ribbon charms and adhere to right side of layout. Mat focal-point photo using dark blue cardstock and light blue cardstocks. Adhere matted photo over patterned paper and left edge of ribbons. Adhere wooden signpost to right side of layout. Trim long strip of printed twill. Smudge blue stamping ink on edges and front of twill. Weave twill through ribbon charm and adhere across layout. Use blue pen for handwritten journaling. Add large blue paperclip to top of layout.

Gemiel Matthews, Yorktown, Virginia

Supplies: Blue cardstocks (Bazzill); patterned paper (Carolee's Creations); ribbon and ribbon charms (Making Memories); wooden sign post (Go West Studios); printed twill (Creative Impressions); ink; blue pen

HULA GIRL

Silk flowers and bright pastels give Melissa's page a feeling of the tropics. Cut sections of blue patterned paper; ink edges and adhere to left side of background. Adhere focal-point photo to right side of page. Print journaling onto transparency and adhere over blue paper. Braid thin strips of raffia and tie ends to create initial for journaling block. Mount onto small square of patterned paper and adhere to journaling block. Ink edges of strip of green patterned paper, stamp title and tie raffia to left end. Attach burlap piece to title strip with brads. Affix letter stickers to burlap. Loosely braid larger raffia to create "curtains." Thread beads onto raffia and use as tie backs for curtains. Attach silk flowers to top of page. Cut "oranges" from patterned paper and ink edges. Print date and place onto transparencies and affix on top of oranges. Ink edges of smaller photos and adhere to page. Ink edges of page.

Melissa Smith, North Richland Hills, Texas

Supplies: Patterned paper and "hula" stamp (Rusty Pickle); letter stickers (Li'l Davis Designs); brads, flowers, raffia, wooden beads; black stamping ink

KATIE

The red background on Karen's two-page layout really makes the black-and-white photos pop. For left page, overlap cut sections of patterned papers; mount to background. Mount photos. Adhere photo with strip across the top. Dye small tag and twill with ink. Stamp message on tag and attach to page. Affix strips stamped with active verbs to right of photos. Adhere small patterned paper square to lower left corner. Insert piece of patterned paper into file folder tab and attach with brads. Adhere definition index tab overlapping patterned paper. Attach brass label holder over index tab with brads. Attach twill to top and bottom of pages using brads. Accent twill with staples and mini safety pins. Place pebbles randomly throughout page. For right page, overlap cut patterned papers and mount along with photos. Affix definition index tab overlapping patterned paper between photos. Affix word strip to right of upper right photo. Dye large tag and twill in walnut ink. Print journaling onto black paper and mount onto large tag. Attach twist-tie and adhere to page. Double-mount wide twill with staples and affix letter stickers. Attach tag to page. Attach brass label holder and twill to page using brads. Accent twill with staples and mini safety pins. Stamp date in center of page. Place pebbles randomly throughout.

Karen Davis, Hillsboro, Ohio

Supplies: Patterned paper (Li'l Davis Designs, Paper Studio, Pebbles); red cardstock (SEI); denim red cardstock (Paper Studio); date stamp (Staples); letter stamps (Hero Arts); twill tape (Creative Impressions); eyelets, flower brads, label holders, mini safety pins, page pebbles (Making Memories); large tag (Avery); small tag (Z International); letter stickers, twist-tie (Pebbles); index tabs (Autumn Leaves); file folder; plain twill tape; staples; tag

DOVE HUNTING DUO

A combination of patterned papers in natural colors complements Tanya's photo of dove-hunting brothers. Tear light green patterned paper along a diagonal and adhere to top right corner of page. Tear thin strips of patterned papers and layer at bottom of page. Accent top and bottom of page with torn dark green strips. Adhere die-cut title to top of page. Mount photo on torn square of red paper and attach brads at corners. Double mount with white and red papers. Wrap hemp around brads and tie in corner. Attach metal accent at bottom center of mat. Wrap hemp around bottom of page. Attach metal letters to vellum tags with brads. Adhere tags and die-cut year to bottom of page.

Tanya Betts, Benson, North Carolina

Supplies: *Patterned papers (Creative Imaginations, Karen Foster Design, Me & My Big Ideas); die-cut letters (Sizzix); hemp twine (Stampin' Up!); metal word, metal-rimmed tags, metal letters (Making Memories); gold and burgundy brads*

HUNTING SEASON

Shannon's page of her brother-in-law's successful hunting trip shares his pride, while her journaling tells of the tradition of fathers and sons hunting together. Crop two photos, mount onto brown cardstock and adhere on background. Stamp along bottom edge and add a strip of brown cardstock. Mount computer-printed border to left side and strips of brown cardstock to top and above large photo. Attach overlay transparency using copper brads. Personalize a faux the vintage record sleeve by stamping a script design on cover. Using a craft knife, cut slits along right side and thread ribbon through holes. Stamp journaling words using black ink. Add a transparency word to the left side. Embellish with zipper and letter buttons. Chalk circle cut-out and add photo. Place journaling block on the back side and sew around sleeve. Secure it on the page, over the transparency using decorative brads.

Shannon Taylor, Bristol, Tennessee

Supplies: *Patterned papers, printed transparency (Karen Foster Design); vintage record sleeve (Anima Designs); script stamp (Inkadinkado); diamond border stamp (Hero Arts); zipper and letter buttons (Junkitz); letter stamps (FontWerks, Hero Arts); decorative brads (Making Memories); brown cardstock; copper brads; ribbon; black and brown stamping inks*

SNOWY OUTLOOK

Silver and white lend a chilly feeling to Denise's page about a snowstorm. Mat patterned paper onto black cardstock background. Print journaling onto transparency; heat emboss. Spray back of transparency with glitter and spray adhesive; adhere to page. Attach rivets to metal paper, paint with acrylic paint and adhere to page with foam adhesive. Attach acrylic tag to top photo and adhere to metal paper. Paint metal clip with silver leafing paint, add word sticker and attach to photo. Stamp date onto strip of cardstock, highlight edges with metallic rub-ons and embellish with brads. Mat large photo with white cardstock and adhere to embossed paper. Attach transparency to photo using vintage buttons and wire. Paint metal strip with white acrylic paint. Sponge silver leafing paint over pattern to highlight and attach to page. To create title, apply rub-on letters to printed vellum. Highlight edges with metallic rub-ons and spray with glitter. Adhere to small white squares and attach to page with foam spacers. Paint back of letter buttons with silver leafing paint. Tie on fiber and adhere to top of page.

Denise Tucker, Versailles, Indiana

Supplies: *Patterned paper (Karen Foster Design); textured paper (Mrs. Grossman's); embossed paper (Provo Craft); printed vellum (Westrim); printed transparency (Artistic Expressions); rub-on letters (Rusty Pickle); embossed metal strip (Making Memories); rivets (Chatterbox); fibers (Yasutomo); metal clip, sticker (Nunn Design); acrylic tag (Go West Studios); glitter spray, silver leafing pen, spray adhesive (Krylon); metallic rub-ons (Craf-T); rubber letter stamps (All Night Media); extra thick embossing powder; brads; letter buttons; vintage buttons; adhesive foam spacers; plain transparency; white acrylic paint*

OUR SKATE DATE

Clean lines and a simple design make Cori's layout look slick. Trim blue cardstock to have a wave at one end. Print journaling on yellow cardstock. Stitch two photos to top of page. Adhere bottom cropped photos to yellow cardstock with adhesive. Stitch cardstock together, overlapping the blue on top of the yellow. Adhere die-cut letters for title to center of page. Stamp date on circle metal-rimmed tag, tie ribbon and attach to page.

Cori Dahmen, Vancouver, Washington

Supplies: *Die-cut letters (QuicKutz); number stamps (Hero Arts); metal-rimmed tag (Office Max); ribbon (Bazzill); yellow and blue cardstocks; black ink*

EGG HUNT

Change is the focus of Ginger's layout about an Easter egg hunt on a beautiful spring day. For left page, trim strip of patterned paper and adhere to center of green cardstock background. Trim strip of lavender cardstock, ink edges and adhere over patterned paper strip. Using image-editing software, print title words onto focal-point photo and adhere. Add additional photos. Print journaling on lavender cardstock, trim and ink edges. Heat emboss mesh squares with assorted pastel colors. Trim egg shapes from cardstock, heat emboss, ink edges and adhere over lavender block. Adhere element to lower right corner. Add decorative white brads to lavender cardstocks. For right page, trim lavender cardstock and heat emboss with assorted pastel colors. Adhere block, patterned paper strips and cardstock strips over background. Adhere photos to top and bottom left corners of page. Cut out and heat emboss egg shapes; attach to page. Heat emboss vellum quote and attach to page over eggs using eyelets. Adhere photos to bottom right corner of page. Write date onto embellished egg. Tie ribbon through eyelet and attach to page.

Ginger McSwain, Cary, North Carolina

Supplies: Patterned paper (Bo-Bunny Press); cardstock (Bazzill); mesh rubber stamp (Hero Arts); vellum quote (DieCuts with a View); ribbon (Offray); oval eyelets (Making Memories)

VALENTINE'S DAY

Simple pink squares give a festive look to Cori's page about Valentine's Day. Adhere patterned paper to white cardstock background and stitch around edges. Print journaling onto vellum and mat photo above. Tear bottom of vellum and adhere to page. Mat additional photos onto hot pink cardstock and adhere. Affix letter stickers to hot pink cardstock to create title. Print remainder of title onto vellum, tear around edges and adhere to title block. Accent with white brads. Attach die-cut cookie to right side of page.

Cori Dahmen, Vancouver, Washington

Supplies: Patterned paper (Paper Fever); letter stickers (KI Memories); die-cut cookie (QuicKutz); brads; hot pink cardstock

LITTLE ELF

A Christmas pageant costume was the inspiration for Polly's holiday page. Sand edges of photos and attach to patterned paper background. Add photos to metal-rimmed tags. Adhere photo tags to aged tags. Stamp date onto one aged tag above photo tag. Stamp journaling onto middle tag, tie ribbon through holes and adhere to page. Adhere quote strip to bottom of page, creating a pocket over rectangular tags. Accent corners with small red buttons. Affix letter stickers and round photo tag to large tag. Attach red ribbon loops to top of large tag. Thread rickrack through loops; affix rickrack and tag to top of page. Attach metal snowflakes to bottom photo and title tag. Accent with red buttons in center. Attach green buttons to red ribbon on large tag. Stamp words onto strip of cream cardstock and attach to page over photo with brads.

Polly McMillan, Bullhead City, Arizona

Supplies: Patterned paper (Imagination Project); aged tags (7 Gypsies); rickrack (Trim-Tex); rubber letter stamps (PSX Design); ribbon (Offray); metal snowflakes (Happy Hammer); metal-rimmed tags (Avery); letter stickers (American Crafts); buttons; quote strip

MY PUMPKIN

Stripes in atypical Halloween colors make the pumpkin photos on Kimberly's page pop. Adhere two large strips of striped patterned paper to middle and right side of light camel cardstock background. Affix photos to page. Journal on strips of white paper and attach to photos along with number stickers. Affix letter stickers and word sticker to white square frame and attach ribbons around the left edge with staples. Adhere frame over small photo, then onto page. Finish with handwritten journaling on patterned paper in top-center block of page.

Kimberly Kesti, Phoenix, Arizona

Supplies: Cardstock (Bazzill); patterned paper (Arctic Frog); letter stickers (Wordsworth); number stickers (Making Memories); word sticker (Pebbles); ribbon (May Arts, Target); photo frame (Memory Lane); journaling pen

SARA TURNS 8

Handmade mini gift bags give an unusual twist to Melissa's birthday page. Trim green cardstock. Mount top and bottom photos onto pink patterned paper and ink edges. Print journaling onto transparency; edge with black ink and adhere over green patterned paper squares and ink-smudged pink cardstock. Affix photo on top of transparency. Smudge edges of two small photos and green cardstock with black ink and attach pink ribbon around corners; mount onto green cardstock. Adhere to pink cardstock section; accent with green gems and small pink bow. Adhere all mounted photos to green cardstock. For mini gift bags, mount small square photos to patterned paper squares smudged with black ink. Wrap top edges with black trim and pink ribbon. Attach tissue paper and "handle" to back of bag. Tie on mini tags and attach to page. Adhere green cardstock to pink patterned paper. Affix letter stickers to side of page to create title. Print onto white cardstock circle, adhere to metal-rimmed circle tag, accent with yellow brad and attach to page. Print stencil number onto patterned paper and cut out with craft knife. Smudge edges with black ink and adhere to black cardstock rectangle. Attach to pink cardstock rectangle and embellish with ribbon and yellow brads. Attach black ribbon to page and smudge ink edges.

Melissa Smith, North Richland Hills, Texas

Supplies: Patterned paper (Reminders of Faith); green patterned paper (Anna Griffin); green cardstock (KI Memories); letter stickers (American Crafts); yellow brads (Making Memories); handles from real shopping bag, metal circle tag, rhinestones, ribbon, tissue paper; foam adhesive spacers

2004 BIRTHDAY

Birthday fun with five friends is the focus of Cori's pretty pink pages. Print journaling onto cardstock and trim into rectangles. Apply rub-on letters above journaling and adhere photos to rectangles. Adhere to pages and machine stitch around edges. For white center rectangle, print journaling onto cardstock, cut and apply rub-on numbers. Stitch to page. Apply rub-on letters to small pink rectangle and stitch to page on top of white rectangle. Affix stickers and rub-ons to larger pink rectangle. Attach silver disc and stitch to page on top of white rectangle. Attach metal flower to page with black brad.

Cori Dahmen, Vancouver, Washington

Supplies: Patterned paper (Keeping Memories Alive); rub-on letters (Making Memories); metal flower (Carolee's Creations); metal disc (Gartner Studios); brad (ScrapArts); sticker words (Boxer Scrapbook Productions); white and pink cardstocks

BIRTHDAY BOY

Becky used black and red as the perfect complement to Adam's shirt. For left page, mount photo onto red cardstock section and mount to tan cardstock background. Affix strip of black cardstock above photo. Add die-cut letters and numbers for age. Attach white label holder to red cardstock with white brads. Adhere small square photos to bottom of page. Apply rub-on word to page and embellish with two white brads in upper left corner. For right page, print journaling onto red cardstock cut into rectangle. Adhere to page. Add strip of black cardstock. Adhere photos to page and embellish with two white brads in lower right corner.

Becky Thompson, Fruitland, Idaho

Supplies: Cardstock (Bazzill); die-cut letters (QuicKutz); brads, rub-on letters, white metal label holder (Making Memories); square punch (Marvy)

SLEEP OVER PARTY

Distressed background paper gives Renee's page the look of a well-used sleeping bag. Wet blue cardstock, crumple and iron. Spray with colorwash and lay flat to dry. If more texture is desired, after spraying with colorwash, crumple again and lay flat to dry. Stitch to page in pattern of five long sections. Mat photos onto black cardstock and add number stickers. Adhere to page. Print journaling onto brown cardstock, cut into square and edge with dark brown distressing ink. Attach A-clip and ribbon and adhere to page. Affix letter stickers to small metal-rimmed tags and attach to page with foam adhesive. Affix black die-cut letters to page and edge page with dark brown distressing ink.

Renee Foss, Seven Fields, Pennsylvania

Supplies: Brown cardstock (Bazzill); ribbon (May Arts); A-clip (7 Gypsies); number stickers (Provo Craft); letter stickers, small metal-rimmed tags (EK Success); die-cut letters (Sizzix); alcohol ink (Ranger); blue cardstock; black cardstock; dark brown distressing ink

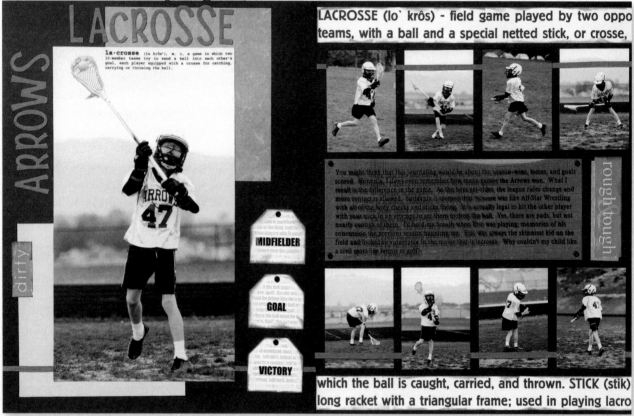

LACROSSE

Kelli captures the excitement and action of lacrosse in this simple two-page layout. For left page, adhere green squares and a thin blue strip to black cardstock background. Affix definition sticker to top of photo and mount photo onto page. Adhere die-cut letters to page to create title. Sand word sticker and smudge with chalk ink. Affix to page. Repeat process with word tags. Affix to page and embellish with black brads. For right page, adhere blue rectangle and small green rectangle to page. Sand and smudge word sticker and adhere over green rectangle. Print journaling onto transparency and attach over blue rectangle with black brads. Adhere photos and thin blue strips to page, weaving strips over and under photos. Affix large definition stickers to page and smudge with chalk inks.

Kelli Noto, Centennial, Colorado

Supplies: *Patterned paper (Carolee's Creations); stickers (Rusty Pickle); word stickers (Pebbles); die-cut letters (QuicKutz); definition sticker (S.R.M.Press); chalk ink (Clearsnap); black and blue cardstocks; transparency; brads*

GAME FACE

Ruthann used this page to highlight the concentration on her son's face during a football game. Mat one photo on black cardstock and adhere to top left of patterned paper background. Adhere all other photos directly to page. Affix transparency, epoxy stickers and page pebbles over photos. Use black pen for handwritten journaling.

Ruthann Grabowski, Yorktown, Virginia

Supplies: Patterned paper, printed transparency, epoxy stickers (Creative Imaginations); black cardstock; pen

MADE TO CHEER

Blue and red perfectly complement Cori's energetic cheerleading layout. Print journaling onto white cardstock background and cover with clear transparency. Adhere blue cardstock to page and mount photos. Attach ribbon to top and bottom edges of cardstock. Tie with smaller ribbons as accents. Add die-cut letters to page for portion of title. Adhere additional die-cut letters to blue circles and to page. Adhere number die cuts to circle for year and attach to bottom of page. Adhere football, flag and megaphone die cuts to bottom of page.

Cori Dahmen, Vancouver, Washington

Supplies: Ribbon (May Arts); circle, football, letter, megaphone, number, pennant die cuts (QuicKutz); dark blue and red cardstock; transparency

Do You Have An Athlete's Foot?

Shoelaces tie the theme of Melisa's layout all together. For left page, adhere thin yellow strip of paper to top of page. Tear black-and-white patterned paper and curl at the edge. Attach eyelets and thread shoestring through. Adhere element to left side of inked background. Attach black eyelets to green patterned paper. Thread ball chain with metal letter tags through and adhere onto backside of page for portion of title. Edge red cardstock rectangle and stamp word with black ink. Stamp title onto yellow cardstock rectangle, smudge with ink and adhere to red rectangle. Edge red cardstock photo mat with ink and mount photo. Attach four black eyelets at bottom and weave yellow patterned paper strip. Secure yellow strip on back side of page. Attach word label to picture. Embellish page with square yellow buttons. For right page, tear black and white patterned paper across and curl at the edge. Adhere to top of inked background. Affix thin yellow strips to top and bottom. Edge red cardstock block with black ink. Attach black eyelets to middle and weave yellow strips in and out. Mount photos to red cardstock and adhere to page. Attach large black brad to upper right corner of rectangle mat. Stamp words onto metal strips with black ink, attach to silver ball chain and wrap around large black brad. Affix silver strips to page and add number bottle caps. Print journaling onto yellow patterned paper, trim, ink edges and adhere. Cut strips of red cardstock and smudge with black ink. Attach black eyelets and thread shoestrings through. Attach to page above and below journaling. Attach word labels to photos and embellish with square yellow buttons.

Melisa Thornton, Munford, Tennessee

Supplies: Patterned paper (KI Memories); red cardstock (Bazzill); small letter stamps (Educational Insights); medium letter stamps (Ma Vinci's Reliquary); large letter stamps and buttons (Making Memories); metal tags (DieCuts With a View); large black eyelets (Prym-Dritz); large silver eyelets (Creative Imaginations); fabric word labels (Me & My Big Ideas); bottle cap numbers (Li'l Davis Designs); silver plant tags (Anima Designs); black ink pad; shoestrings; silver ball chains

Good Sport

Kathe used a variety of black, blue and white patterned papers to capture the energy of a successful soccer season. Adhere patterned paper with small numbers to black cardstock. Tear patterned paper with large numbers diagonally and affix on one corner of page. Stamp number and journal onto white cardstock. Cut and mount onto black cardstock and adhere to page. Cut strips of striped paper, mount on strips of black cardstock and attach to page over white cardstock piece. Mount all photos onto black cardstock and adhere to page. Embellish with chipboard words.

Kathe Cunningham, Buford, Georgia

Supplies: Cardstock (Bazzill); patterned paper (Creative Imaginations); chipboard words (Li'l Davis Designs); rubber stamp (Purple Onion Designs); chalk ink (Clearsnap); pen

TOTAL FOCUS

Kim coordinated her layout using both color and black-and-white photos with muted gray tones in the papers. Ink edges of brick-red background. Trim strips of patterned paper and sand edges. Adhere the center block to background. Fold the striped paper horizontally and the circle paper into small sections. Sand the folded edges and adhere to background. Sew a straight stitch around the edges of the three blocks and a zigzag stitch between. Trim a piece of patterned paper and adhere near upper right corner. Ink edges of a metal frame and mount it with photo. Add focal-point photo and secondary photo matted on black cardstock. Create and apply labels. Create a folded journaling element with two photos on the front and journaling inside. Adhere to page. Create title using letter stickers and letter stamps.

Kim Mattina, Phoenix, Arizona

Supplies: *Patterned papers (Mustard Moon); epoxy stickers (Creative Imaginations); letter stamps (Ma Vinci's Reliquary); black solvent ink (Tsukineko); label maker (Dymo); metal frame (Making Memories); tan and red cardstocks*

PUMPED, PROUD, PLEASED

Fabric and embroidery floss give the impression of an actual baseball on Denise's layout. Trim fabric, fray edges and swipe with acrylic paint. Adhere to black cardstock background. Pierce holes into cardstock and stitch baseball pattern with red embroidery floss. Double mount strip of patterned paper onto red and black papers. Adhere to page with foam adhesive. Crumple brown cardstock and iron flat. Coat with decoupage medium to create the look of leather. Punch small holes and thread hemp into "X" pattern. Mount photo onto brown cardstock with foam adhesive, then mount onto black cardstock. Create title by attaching tags to paper and running through a printer. Heat emboss, ink edges and attach charms. Affix to page. Print journaling and "scoreboard" onto transparencies and adhere to page.

Denise Tucker, Versailles, Indiana

Supplies: *Patterned paper (Rusty Pickle); tags (Pebbles); charms (Beadery); transparency (Artistic Expressions); decoupage medium (Plaid); extra thick embossing powder (Ranger); spray adhesive (Krylon); black ink; acrylic paint; embroidery thread; fabric, hemp; foam adhesive*

LAKERIDGE TRACK

Team colors are the basis for this simple layout about Teresa's daughter's track season. Slightly bend faux cardboard paper and adhere to page; accent with pewter brads. Affix large and small black-and-white letter stickers to create title. Mount photos on white cardstock and adhere. Print journaling on faux cardboard, cut into strip and attach to page with staples. Edge small envelope with brown ink and adhere to page; accent with pewter brad. Attach small eyelets to page on either side of envelope. Thread red cord through in an "X" pattern and tie. Print journaling onto cardstock and slip into envelope.

Teresa Snyder, Orem, Utah

Supplies: Patterned paper, small black and white alphabet stickers and cardstock (Pebbles); large alphabet stickers (Sicker Studio); pewter brads, red cording, staples (Making Memories); envelope; eyelets

GET YOUR GAME ON

Becky's son's first hockey season is highlighted with nontraditional colors such as terra cotta, brown and tan. Affix letter stickers to page to create title. Print quotes onto transparency, cut into strips and adhere to page. Cut out black cardstock circle and stamp letters using cranberry paint. Once dry, adhere to page. Adhere photos to page. Print journaling onto transparency, trim and attach to page over title stickers. Edge bottom corners of overlay transparency with brown ink and attach to page.

Becky Heisler, Waupaca, Wisconsin

Supplies: Patterned paper (Autumn Leaves); black cardstock (Bazzill); transparency (Sweetwater); stickers (American Crafts); rubber stamp (Stamp Craft); distress ink (Ranger); acrylic paint

CHEETAH GIRL

Wooden letters and polka-dot paper give Angelia's page about sports a fresh and unique look. Adhere polka-dot patterned paper to blue cardstock section. Attach brads and wooden letters to pale blue cardstock strip and adhere above patterned paper. Affix letter stickers to light blue cardstock strip and attach to page. Mount four small photos to pale blue cardstock and adhere to page. Print journaling onto red cardstock, trim and attach black tab with brads; adhere to page. Mount single photo onto pale blue cardstock and attach above journaling. Affix large number stickers to bottom of journaling block. Accent with small printed pieces of cardstock.

Angelia Wigginton, Belmont, Mississippi

Supplies: Patterned paper, large number stickers (American Crafts); cardstock (Bazzill); black letter stickers (Doodlebug Design); wooden letters (Li'l Davis Designs); black tab (7 Gypsies); mini brads (Making Memories)

MY PERFECT 10

Tricia combined grunge-style letters, a sports transparency and inking with the softness of plaid fabric patterned paper to highlight the sweet face and action photos of her gymnast daughter. Trim patterned papers and arrange on black cardstock background. Mat focal-point color photo on black cardstock and adhere. Add remaining photos, trim the sports transparency and adhere over photos. Create three tags. Add a reinforcement, ribbon and rub-on letters. Stamp numeral on a largest tag; add rub-on letters and ribbon. Print journaling onto a third tag and add ribbon. Ink all tags and adhere them to the page. Add date label and sticker border.

Tricia Rubens, Castle Rock, Colorado

Supplies: Patterned papers (Art Impressions, Daisy D's, Rusty Pickle); rub-on letters (Rusty Pickle); foam number stamps (Making Memories); cream tags (Avery); red gingham ribbon (Michaels); gymnastics transparency, champion sticker (Daisy D's); label maker (Dymo); small tag punch (Marvy); red acrylic paint; black cardstock; green stamping ink

Much to their chagrin, parents will kiss their kids in front of classmates, address them with pet names like Lulabell or Doodlebug, sing made-up songs and tell the same stories over and over. There are no limits to the ways parents express their love to their one-of-a-kind kid—no matter how much it embarrasses them. But kids are smart and no degree of humiliation will ever let them forget that the smooches, silly names and standard lectures translate into unconditional, melt-your-heart, I-love-you-forever kind of love. It is through this unconditional love that kids develop their own sense of self and learn to love the people and things that define them as unique individuals. As they grow older and more independent, kids quickly learn to express their own personal sense of style, show their undying love for pets and crave their favorite foods, toys and games. And through butterfly kisses and the tender words of "I love you," they affirm the love they have for their parents, siblings and other family members, making the love they have for each other the greatest love of all.

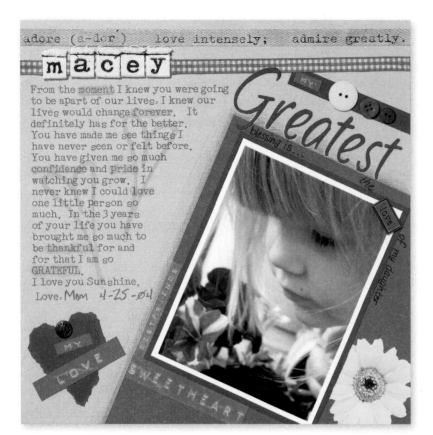

MACEY

Contrasting colors and watercolor pencil accent Jennifer's layout perfectly. Mat photo onto purple cardstock. Print journaling onto green cardstock background. Cut red cardstock into geometric shape to line up with bottom corner. Adhere matted photo to red cardstock, then adhere element to page. Affix twill tape sticker along top of page. Weave ribbon through fabric letters and attach to page. Adhere small strip of purple cardstock. Affix label sticker and embellish with buttons. Print title onto purple cardstock, cut out with a craft knife and adhere to page. Finish title by writing on red cardstock. Embellish photo with pewter charm, label stickers and flower. Tear a heart shape from purple cardstock. Adhere to page and accent with pewter brad. Add label stickers. Shade around photo and over key words in journaling with watercolor pencil.

Jennifer Lamb, Rolesville, North Carolina

Supplies: Cardstock (Bazzill); twill tape sticker, label stickers (Pebbles); heart rubber stamp (Sugarloaf Products); watermark stamp pad (Tsukineko); red gingham ribbon (Close To My Heart); copper brads, buttons (Making Memories); watercolor pencils (Staedtler); flower sticker (Cropper Hopper); pewter metal accents (K & Company); twill letters (Carolee's Creations); journaling pen

CONVERSATIONS WITH DANE

A conversation full of innocent questions between Rachael and her son was the inspiration for this layout. Print journaling on red cardstock, trim vertically. Apply rub-on letters for title. Attach to patterned paper. Mount photo onto black cardstock and attach to right side of page. Wrap ribbon around top and bottom edges and across right side.

Rachael Giallongo, Auburn, New Hampshire

Supplies: Patterned paper (MOD-my own design); red cardstock (Bazzill); rub-on letters (Making Memories); ribbon (Offray)

WHAT I WISH FOR YOU

Asian characters and plum-colored cardstock give a peaceful, flowing feeling to Barbara's page about growing up. Adhere patterned paper to tan cardstock background. Tear plum cardstock and adhere to left side of page. Affix Chinese character stickers and black border sticker. Print journaling on plum cardstock. Trim into a square, affix border stickers and attach to page. Adhere photos, overlapping plum square. Apply rub-on letters and letter stickers to create title at bottom of page.

Barbara Oyer, Lansing, Michigan

Supplies: Patterned paper (Provo Craft); border stickers (Mrs. Grossman's); Chinese character stickers (Crafts, Etc.); letter stickers (Creative Imaginations); rub-on letters (Making Memories)

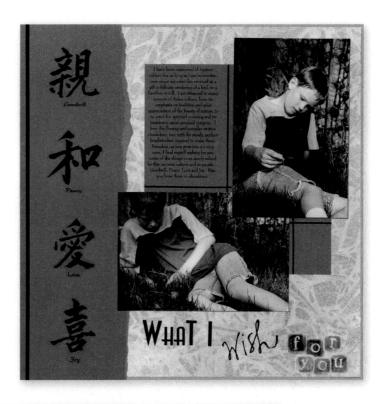

OCEAN BREEZES

Double sheets of cardstock attached with foam adhesive give a three-dimensional look to Denise's page about a day at the beach. Crumple one sheet of patterned paper. Flatten and iron. Swipe white acrylic paint onto page randomly to create a "dreamy" effect. Tear a circle from center of patterned paper. Back page with cardstock for added firmness. Print journaling onto transparency and heat emboss. Adhere to bottom sheet of patterned paper. Mat photo onto white cardstock and apply rub-on letters. Affix round gold stickers to edge of photo and punch holes in their centers. Thread ribbon through and attach photo to page. Affix small painting sticker to a small piece of white cardstock. Affix frame sticker over painting. Attach small tag with a safety pin. Print title onto cardstock and cut out with a craft knife. Mat, re-cut and adhere to page with foam adhesive. Embellish with seashells and corner stickers.

Denise Tucker, Versailles, Indiana

Supplies: Patterned paper, frames, photo corners, silk hand-dyed ribbon, painting sticker (Paper House Productions); rub-ons letters, tag (Westrim); safety pin (Making Memories); metallic rub-ons (Craft-T); shells; acrylic paint; transparency; embossing powder; foam adhesive

IS THIS THE LOOK

Jenn captured her son's unique facial expression in this digital layout. Applying several layers, add digital papers to the right side of canvas. Add a drop shadow on each for definition. Open a text box over the brown paper and type journaling. Add date to the bottom block. Open photo and crop, if needed. Arrange it on the left side of the page. Type title on top and add ribbon and metal ring.

Jenn Brookover, San Antonio, Texas

Supplies: Image-editing software (Adobe Photoshop 2.0); Rhonna Farrer ribbon, overlay and monogram (www.twopeasinabucket.com); papers and metal embellishments (www.thedigichick.com)

is this the look...

that you'll give your teacher when your homework isn't done?

that you'll show me when you wreck my car for the first time?

that you'll have when you ask your girlfriend to become your wife?

that you'll pass on to your son one day?

that will remain a perfect memory in my heart forever.

[11 20 04]

BEAUTIFUL

g i r l

WHEN YOU LOOK IN HER EYES THE FUTURE LOOKS BRIGHT!

LAUREN

2 0 0 3

BEAUTIFUL GIRL

Silk flowers perfectly complement this photo of Polly's daughter in a tropical setting. Tear patterned paper and adhere to top of page. Attach photo. Stamp title on top of patterned paper. Affix tag stickers to circle metal-rimmed tags, adhere to silk daisies and attach to page. Stamp journaling onto small strips of patterned paper and adhere to page. Thread yellow silk flowers onto yellow gingham ribbon and attach. Stamp year at bottom of page. Add flower sticker embellishment.

Polly McMillan, Bullhead City, Arizona

Supplies: Patterned paper and die-cut stickers (Doodlebug Design); stamps (PSX Design); ribbon (Offray); round tags (Making Memories); silk flowers

IN YOUR EYES

Colleen's page features photos of her son's striking blue eyes and journaling that tells her story of some of her life decisions. Create a color-blocked background by adhering a light blue strip of patterned paper across the top, a larger block of light blue swirl paper below on the right and a striped block on the left. Apply mesh across the top of page. Using image-editing software, add a text box to the focal-point photo for the title. Print photo and mat onto blue cardstock. Add photo corners and adhere to layout. Print journaling on transparency, trim and mount over striped paper. Double mat medium photo and embellish with ribbon. Ink edges of a microscope slide with blue ink and position over smallest photo. Use letter die stamps to stamp child's name onto plant tag and adhere to bottom of layout.

Colleen Stearns,
Natrona Heights, Pennsylvania

Supplies: Image-editing software (Adobe Photoshop Elements); patterned papers, photo corners and letter die stamps (Making Memories); blue solvent ink (Tsukineko); blue mesh (Magic Scraps); microscope slide (Scrapping With Style); organza ribbon (May Arts); plant tag (Jest Charming); blue cardstock

IN HER HEART

Inspired by a magazine advertisement, Mellette created this page featuring numbered journaling that she printed directly on a trio of photos. Open photo in image-editing software and add a text box. Type numbers and change color to orange. Create another text box, type text and change to white. Arrange boxes so that text is layered over numbers. Print photos and adhere to background. Print title and date on vellum block. Punch square to reveal patterned paper beneath. Trim a cardstock frame and adhere over vellum element. Add metal charms, ribbon and floss.

Mellette Berezoski, Crosby, Texas

Supplies: Patterned paper (Chatterbox); flower charm (www.twopeasinabucket.com); square punch (Marvy); heart charm (Making Memories); image-editing software (Adobe Photoshop); orange silk ribbon; yellow cardstock; orange floss; vellum

MARIAH AT 9

A window mount gives a unique look into the traits that represent Wendy's daughter at age nine. Edge various patterned border stickers with black ink and affix in a row. Mount photo onto black-and-white patterned paper, edge with black ink and adhere on top of border stickers. Accent with letter sticker and ribbon. Trim border stickers and apply randomly to form collage in bottom corner. Stamp words onto stickers. Embellish with number sticker, buttons, charms, ribbon and stamped expressions. Color window mount with metallic rub-ons and tie three ribbons to one side. Attach metal letter and die-cut word to complete title.

Wendy Inman, Virginia Beach, Virginia
Photo: Teresa Olier, Colorado Springs, Colorado

Supplies: *Patterned paper (Deluxe Designs, 7 Gypsies); cardstock (Bazzill); metal letter, stickers, window mount (Deluxe Designs); ribbon (May Arts); button (Bazzill); washer (Making Memories); rubber stamps (PSX Design); sticker (Flair Designs); metallic rub-ons (Craft-T)*

10 THINGS I LOVE ABOUT YOU

The bright color of Jill's daughter's shirt was the inspiration for this cheery layout. Cut strips of various patterned papers and adhere vertically over white cardstock background. Trim large block of white cardstock and adhere. Print words onto additional pieces of white cardstock, trim to form file tabs and adhere to page. Attach large block of green vellum across center of layout. Staple ribbons to top of vellum. Print phrases onto white paper, cut into strips and adhere to green vellum. Attach photo to page. Print letters for child's name onto white cardstock and cut out with a craft knife. Color in with markers and adhere to page. Cut thin strips of coordinating ribbons, adhere to page and accent with button. Embellish page with colorful buttons.

Jill Jackson-Mills, Roswell, Georgia

Supplies: *Patterned paper (K & Company); buttons (Making Memories); ribbon (Offray); letters (Michaels); green pastel vellum (Hot Off The Press); white cardstock*

GROWING UP

Inspired by the photos of her son, Marcee created a digital layout with an artsy but masculine feel. For a modified photo background, open photo in image-editing software and crop. Using a downloadable plug-in, open the Virtual Photographer and choose Color › Ambience. Fill new layer with white. Use the eraser tool with a chalk brush to erase the center, leaving only the edges of white over the photo. Change the opacity of the white layer to 50 percent. Under the layer menu choose Merge Visible to combine the layers. Add the modified photo to a new 12 x 12" layer filled with yellow. Create a grunge background using brushes with the Dodge and Burn commands. Add text, changing color and size where needed.

Marcee Duggar, Glen Saint Mary, Florida

Supplies: *Image-editing software (Adobe Photoshop 7); Growing Up digital kit (www.digitalscrapbookplace.com); Virtual Photographer (www.optikvervelabs.com)*

ONE OF A KIND

Suzy captures the beauty of being a unique person in this layout of rust, white and blue papers. Attach patterned paper to left side of blue background. Cut a circle from white paper and adhere to page. Attach photos at an angle and affix label stickers to corner of each. Draw "wave" shape on white cardstock, cut out and adhere to bottom of page. Print journaling onto cardstock. Cut into a square and adhere to bottom of page at end of wave. Embellish with two white brads. Affix stickers to top of page for title. Draw arrow onto cardstock, cut out and adhere to top of page.

Suzy West, Fremont, California

Supplies: *Patterned paper (Mustard Moon); cardstock (Chatterbox); letter stickers (KI Memories); label maker (Dymo); brads*

LOVE YOU

To mimic the trees in her backyard, Jlyne applied a translucent sticker overlay of cracking paint over patterned paper. Trim charcoal gray paper and adhere to black cardstock background. Crop patterned paper and crackle sticker. Layer paper, photo, overlay and word sticker. Apply rub-on letters for quote and additional word. Cover the seam with gingham ribbon. Add photo corners.

Jlyne Hanback, Biloxi, Mississippi

Supplies: Patterned papers, sticker overlay, love sticker (Tumblebeasts); rub-on letters, quote (Chatterbox); self-adhesive pewter photo corners; gingham ribbon; black cardstock

MY RAY OF SUNSHINE

To highlight her daughter's golden hair and sparkling face, Angela created a digital layout using a page kit she downloaded. Open photo into image-editing software and crop. Download a "kit" of elements for the page including papers, love ribbon and tag. Embellish page as desired. Create tag pull and add to tag. Add journaling by opening a text box. Change the font and enlarge a few words for emphasis. Create a black mat around the photo by adding a stroke layer. Add depth to page elements by defining layer styles for drop shadows.

Angela Svoboda, Ord, Nebraska

Supplies: Image-editing software (Adobe Photoshop Creative Suite); free digital page kit (www.digitaldesignessentials.com)

WALK TALL SIERRA

A special song was the inspiration for Suzy's page. Print journaling onto pink cardstock, trim and adhere to right side of patterned paper background. Embellish journaling block with painted metal molding strip, paisley patterned paper, lace and decorative brad. Add black-and-white photo to lower left corner of layout. Stamp portion of title with green acrylic paint onto background. Attach flower and letter stickers to complete title. Trim two strips of paisley patterned paper and adhere around title. Affix letter stickers for name at bottom.

Suzy West, Fremont, California

Supplies: Patterned paper (Daisy D's); letter stickers (KI Memories); brads, molding strip, stamps (Making Memories); paint; ribbon, flower

SENSITIVE SWEET ROBBY

To enhance the rich orange of her son's sweater, Shannon used retro papers on brown cardstock. Trim retro patterned papers and layer onto brown cardstock background. Stitch borders using brown embroidery floss. Mat photo onto brown cardstock and adhere. Trim orange ribbons and adhere. Flatten bottle caps, add letter and number stickers and mount at ends of ribbon. Affix letter stickers to create title words.

Shannon Taylor, Bristol, Tennessee

Supplies: Patterned papers, bottle caps, bottle cap stickers and letter stickers (Mustard Moon); brown embroidery floss (DMC); ribbon (Rusty Pickle)

IT'S YOU I LIKE

Becky cleverly uses a poem for her journaling on this page about her daughter. Print poem onto brown card-stock background. Affix sections of patterned paper and green cardstock to page. Adhere photo on top of green section. Color hearts and eyelet with copper leafing pen. Attach strand of beads to top of green section and hearts to the bottom. Affix slide mount embellished with eyelets and buttons over select letter.

Becky Thompson, Fruitland, Idaho

Supplies: Patterned paper (Deluxe Designs); buttons (Making Memories); slide mount (Loersch); beaded wire (Creative Imaginations); copper leafing pen (Krylon); eyelet; metal heart brad

UNCONDITIONAL LOVE

The colors of this layout exude peace and complement Mary's black-and-white photos. Layer blue cardstock, patterned papers and photos over yellow cardstock background. Print journaling on yellow cardstock, trim and adhere. Apply rub-on letters and letter stickers to create title. Print quote on green cardstock, trim into strip and adhere. Attach gingham ribbon and silk flower with brad over quote. Print name on strip of green cardstock and attach over focal-point photo with decorative brads. Print definition onto small strip of white cardstock, smudge with yellow ink and adhere. Trim a small strip of patterned paper, attach over journaling block and embellish with safety pin, letter sticker and poemstone sticker .

Mary Faith Roell, Harrison, Ohio

Supplies: Patterned paper (Chatterbox); flower, gingham ribbon, safety pin (Making Memories); poemstone (Creative Imaginations); quote (Foofala); letter stickers (EK Success)

THAT'S MY BOY

Kelie used a unique method for her hidden journaling by adhering it to a traditional library card. Stamp name onto inked burgundy cardstock background using foam letter stamps and acrylic paint. Layer black, cream and lime green cardstocks with photos and preprinted transparencies. Affix definition sticker to library pocket, adhere to bottom of page beneath photo and add large paper clip. Print journaling on lime green cardstock, trim and smudge edges with pigment ink; add handwritten signature and stamped title. Adhere journaling block to stamped library card; embellish with burgandy cardstock, washer and ribbon. Embellish page with definition file card, word stickers, decorative brads, woven fabric label, letter pebbles, printed twill, metal ransom letters, black label and ribbon.

Kelie Myers, Tahlequah, Oklahoma

Supplies: Cardstock (Prism, Stampin' Up!); letter stamps (EK Success, Hero Arts, Stampin' Up!); mini date stamp (Ideal); foam letter stamps, definition sticker, metal letter (Making Memories); stickers (Pebbles); ribbon (Offray); black label (Dymo); woven label (Me & My Big Ideas); file card (Autumn Leaves); rivets (Chatterbox); metal stencil letter (Colorbök); transparency (Creative Imaginations); acrylic paint; pigment ink; washer; letter; pebbles; date stamp; staples; twill tape; large paper clip

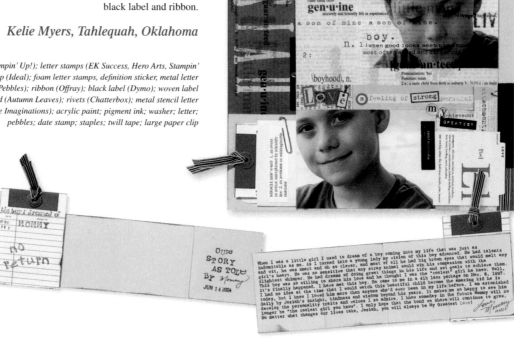

BELIEVE IN YOURSELF

A skeleton leaf adds the feeling of nature to Margaret's page celebrating her son. Cut various sections of patterned papers. On one section, punch hole and tie gingham ribbon. Crop focal-point photo, punch hole and tie gingham ribbon. Print name on dark brown cardstock and trim. Layer papers, cardstocks and photo and adhere to light brown cardstock background. Print journaling on two pieces of beige cardstock, trim and stitch together with black embroidery floss. Splatter envelope with brown ink and attach heart and inked twill ribbon. Adhere element to page. Heat emboss punched metal letter and metal word; adhere to page. Apply rub-on letters to create title. Embellish page with metal words, inked definition sticker, border sticker, brads and skeleton leaf.

Margaret Winters, Wichita, Kansas

Supplies: Patterned paper (Hot Off The Press, K & Company, SEI); brad letter stickers, definition stickers, mini brads, metal words, rub-on letters (Making Memories); skeleton leaf (Leaving Prints); punched metal letter (Colorbök); metal accents (K & Company); embossing powder; twill ribbon; gingham ribbon; cardstock; envelope; brown stamping ink

FAVORITES

The variety of blue patterned papers on Polly's page makes the black-and-white photo pop. Tear polka-dot paper diagonally and adhere to page. Cut a strip of polka-dot paper and adhere to top of page. Add title letters. Tear right side of photo and attach to page, embellishing with photo corners. Cut a section of blue square paper, tear at bottom and tie ribbon around top. Affix to page. Stamp two large tags and embellish with sticker and drawing. Stamp word onto small square of patterned paper. Affix small label onto scrap of paper and adhere to small square. Adhere both to tag. Attach spiral clip, tie ribbon to all tags and adhere. Stamp words onto small strips of paper and tear ends. Adhere two strips to two small tags and embellish with ribbons. Adhere three strips of paper at bottom. Cover round metal-rimmed tags with patterned paper after stamping onto one. Embellish with heart clip and heart die cut. Embellish page with photo corners.

Polly McMillan, Bullhead City, Arizona

Supplies: Patterned paper (KI Memories, Pebbles); title letters (Remember When); ribbon (Offray); small tags, metal-rimmed tags (Avery); large tags (DMD); heart punch (EK Success); decorative paper clips (Making Memories); letter stamps (PSX Design); label maker (Dymo); photo corners (3L)

THE ESSENTIALS

As Kimberly set up an in-home studio to take a portrait of her son, he grabbed the three items he treasures most. She featured her favorite enlarged photo with simple elements to round out the page. Enlarge photo and mount on page. Print journaling on green cardstock and use as background. Trim striped paper and adhere a border along the bottom and a block in the upper-left corner. Adhere photo and add title stickers to complete.

Kimberly Lund, Wichita, Kansas

Supplies: Striped paper (K & Company); letter stickers (EK Success, Pebbles); green cardstock

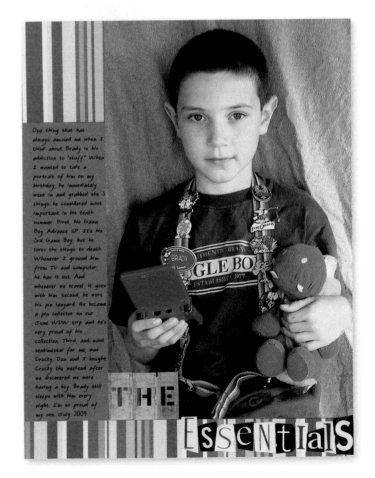

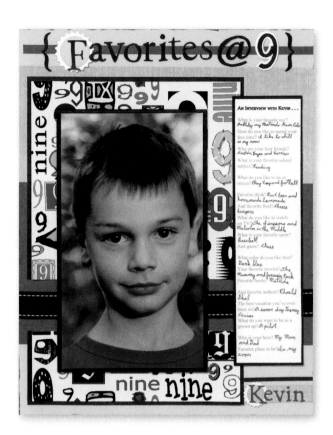

FAVORITES @ 9

Kelli called upon the talents of her son to create this bright and funky page about his favorites. Kevin designed the title and used image-editing software to create the "nine" paper. Crop bright blocks of paper and place horizontally on page. Ink around the outer edge of the page. Open a blank document in image-editing software. Type "nine" and "9" around page. Change fonts, colors, sizes and add shapes for interest. Print and mount on black cardstock. Adorn with a piece of red cardstock and ribbon. Mount photo using foam adhesive. Print questions. Have child handwrite answers. Mat onto black paper and adhere. Handcut @ symbol. Add die-cut title, name and bottle caps.

Kelli Noto, Centennial, Colorado

Supplies: *Green patterned paper (Carolee's Creations); letter die cuts, bottle cap die cuts (QuicKutz); image-editing software (Adobe Photoshop); black, yellow, red and white cardstocks; ribbon; black stamping ink; foam adhesive; black pen*

PLAYFULNESS

Classic primary colors give Angie's layout a fun feeling. For left page, cut strips of red and yellow cardstocks and adhere to top and bottom of blue cardstock background. Mat large photo on yellow cardstock, embellish with rub-on word and adhere to page. Embellish top and bottom borders with star snaps. For right page, cut strips of red and yellow cardstock and adhere to top and bottom of background. Embellish top and bottom borders with star snaps. Align and mount smaller photos. Print words onto photos using image-editing software. Adhere small photos in two columns of three. Print journaling onto transparency and adhere to page over small photos. Stamp date in bottom left corner.

Angie Head, Friendswood, Texas

Supplies: *Paper, letter stamps and rub-on words (Making Memories); cardstock (Bazzill); star snaps (Chatterbox); spray adhesive (Krylon); transparency*

KELSEY FAVORITES AT 5

Preserving the memory of some of her daughter's favorite things is the subject of Kathryn's layout. Tear top of patterned paper and adhere to black cardstock background. Create tags from beige cardstock and affix rub-on letters. Embellish with ribbon and adhere to page. Stamp words onto small strip of patterned paper. Adhere to page with silver brads. Paint metal number with acrylic paint, attach to page and affix watch crystal on top. Mat photo on torn cardstock and adhere to page. Attach metal number to bottom of photo. Print journaling onto small rectangle of beige cardstock. Mat on torn cardstock and attach with brads. Adhere thin strip of vellum to bottom of page and attach metal flower plaque. Thread beads onto coated linen thread and attach to page with small black brads.

Kathryn Allen, Hamilton, Ohio

Supplies: *Patterned paper (Creative Imaginations, PSX Design); metal plaque, metal number, ribbon, rub-on letters (Making Memories); rubber stamps (Hero Arts); beads, coated linen thread (Close To My Heart); watch crystal*

LUCKY

Jessie put together some of her daughter's collection of bottle caps, or "luckies," on background paper with a grid pattern. Using word processing software, type journaling, fill box with black; change text to white. Print, trim black paper into a horizontal strip and adhere to page. Attach a garment label with a black brad. Mount photo. Apply rub-on letters to bottle caps to create title. Adhere caps along with collected ones using foam adhesive. Use the block pattern on the background paper as a placement guide.

Jessie Baldwin, Las Vegas, Nevada

Supplies: *Patterned paper (Paper Loft); blank bottle caps (Design Originals); rub-on letters (Making Memories); foam adhesive; Lucky Brand garment tag; printed bottle caps (from Violet's collection); black brad*

SLIPPERS

Her daughter's love for these slippers inspired Ralonda to feature graphic patterned paper in dusty pinks and greens. Trim papers to be arranged in a color-blocked pattern and ink edges. Dry-brush paint the edges of the focal-point photo and adhere. Add acrylic word tag to lower right corner of photo and secure with brads. Hand sew a zigzag pattern with embroidery floss as shown. Affix the smaller photo and add a metal frame embellished with ribbons. Embellish with ribbons and acrylic word tag. Print journaling block, ink edges and adhere. Handcut title letters, ink edges and adhere to top of page.

Ralonda Heston, Murfreesboro, Tennessee

Supplies: Patterned papers (Imagination Project); green metal frame (Making Memories); ribbons (Fibers By The Yard, May Arts); acrylic words (Go West Studios); green embroidery floss (Prym-Dritz); watermark ink (Tsukineko); green brads; white acrylic paint

SARA AND BABY LILY

Melissa captures the special bond between a little girl and her doll in this layout with soft pinks, lavenders and greens. Smudge edges of patterned paper background with black solvent ink. Print words onto vellum and cut into tag shapes. Paint underside of tags with beige acrylic paint and smudge edges with purple. Embellish with ribbons and attach to page. Affix ampersand sticker. Handcut name from cardstock; add dimension with clear embossing powder. Rub edges with black solvent ink and attach to page. Doublemat photo onto cardstock and rub edges with black solvent ink. Cut along flower pattern on paper and insert corner of photo. Adhere photo to page and embellish with flower cut from paper and silk leaves. Print journaling onto cardstock, edge with purple acrylic paint and adhere. Embellish with decorative brad and silk flower. Cut strip of purple cardstock, edge with black solvent ink, wrap around metal hanger and adhere. Affix small photos at top and bottom. Paint slide mounts with acrylic paint. Print date onto transparency. Weave thin ribbon in and out of holes at top. Adhere pieces of transparency to back of slide mounts and attach to page over small photos. Embellish with decorative brads, silk flowers and small epoxy letters.

Melissa Smith, North Richland Hills, Texas

Supplies: Patterned paper, butterfly metal hanger, metal frames, small epoxy letters (K & Company); sticker (Creative Imaginations); metal brads (Making Memories); black solvent ink (Tsukineko); embossing powder; ribbon; beige and purple acrylic paint; transparency

YOUR PERSONAL SENSE OF STYLE

Karen's son's sense of style is expressed with many patterns papers. Cut rectangles from patterned papers and layer at random over brown cardstock background. Double mat photo on tan and red inked cardstocks and adhere to page. Tie ribbons onto metal tags and attach to photo mat. Mat second photo onto red cardstock; adhere to page and embellish with red glass squares. Print journaling onto transparency, trim and adhere over patterned paper square. Attach both to page, fitting photo between paper and transparency. Print title onto transparency and affix over strip of patterned paper. Affix letter tags and label to page. Stamp word onto small strip of cardstock and adhere to page; attach label holder over word and secure with brads.

Karen Huntoon,
East Longmeadow, Massachusetts

Supplies: Patterned paper (Li'l Davis Designs, Provo Craft, Rusty Pickle, 7 Gypsies); cardstock (Bazzill); stickers (Rusty Pickle); letter stamps (PSX Design); brads, metal alphabet tags (Making Memories); label holder (KI Memories); label maker (Dymo); ribbon (Textured Trio); glass squares (Michaels); black ink

FASHION STATEMENT

Tammy's layout emphasizes the innocent "fashion sense" of a 6-year-old. Brush white cardstock background with green paint. Affix mesh to background with glue adhesive. Double mat top photo with dark green and black cardstocks and adhere. Mat bottom photo onto dark green cardstock and adhere over mesh. Create title using letter stickers and brads. Affix small photo to square metal-rimmed tag. Attach wire through hole in tag and wrap around letter brad. Print journaling onto dark green cardstock and adhere to page.

Tammy McLaughlin, Meansville, Georgia

Supplies: Cardstock (DMD); letter stickers (Provo Craft); letter brads (Li'l Davis Designs); metal-rimmed tag (Making Memories); green paint; black cardstock; white cardstock; mesh

Now

Shona's page perfectly captures the essence of Amber's spirit at age 12. Ink edges of beige cardstock background. Adhere patterned paper to middle of background. Stamp corners with foam stamp and black paint. Affix red ribbon at top and bottom of patterned paper. Mat photo on inked beige cardstock and adhere. Print journaling onto transparency; adhere to page next to photo. Attach red cardstock to back of letter stencil letters and adhere to top and bottom of page. Embellish transparency with square brads painted red. Stamp date onto page.

Shona Iverson, Saskatoon, Saskatchewan, Canada

Supplies: Patterned paper (Daisy D's); cardstock (Bazzill); stencils (Autumn Leaves); ribbon (Textured Trios); foam stamps, paint (Making Memories); square brads (Creative Impressions); date stamp (Trodat); distress ink (Ranger); transparency

Fashion is General

Laura used photocopies of clothing tags from some of her daughter's favorite brands on this page about her current likes. Cut strips of coordinating patterned papers and adhere to cardstock background in an overlapping, horizontal pattern. Mat photo onto pink cardstock and attach to page. Print journaling onto vellum, mat onto green cardstock. Embellish with snaps and adhere to page. Fold green patterned paper to create a pocket. Tie pink and green fabric strips and pearls around pocket and attach to page. Photocopy clothing tags and affix on outside and inside of pocket. Apply letter stickers to dog tag, tie pearls through hole and attach to page. Stamp quote on patterned paper strips. Embellish with pink folios on left side of page.

Laura Swinson, Pearland, Texas

Supplies: Patterned paper, letter stickers and nails (Chatterbox); small letter stamps (Hero Arts); large letter stamps (EK Success); pink folios (Colorbök); metal tag (Magic Scraps); pearl strand (Fibers By The Yard); pink and green fabric, photocopied clothing tags

LOVE CHOCOLATE

Chris used pink and brown papers to highlight Zane's "sweet" love of chocolate. Cut patterned paper into thin strip and large rectangle section; adhere over brown cardstock background. Enlarge and print photo onto beige cardstock; adhere to right side of page. Adhere color photo to page. Mount small square of patterned paper onto cardstock smudged with brown chalk. Print journaling onto pink paper, cut out and adhere over square. Attach element to page. Handcut letters out of pink cardstock for title, smudge with brown chalk and attach to page. Fold chocolate bar wrappers and attach to page at top of square with staples. Embellish page with patterned paper blocks, staples and label.

Chris Eckert, Gilbert, Arizona

Supplies: Patterned paper, chalks, die-cut rectangle (Deluxe Designs); cardstock (Bazzill); label maker (Dymo); staples

JIMMY LOVES CHOCOLATE MILK

Wanda created a hip digital page featuring the colors found in her grandson's cup. Using image-editing software, crop and size photos. Create a new 12 x 12" document canvas and place photos. Using a plug-in filter, create borders around the photos. Open a text box, choose fonts and type journaling over bottom left photo. Add a transparency filter to the letters. Select font, type title and apply a drop shadow in white. Type additional words and add an even transparency filter to lighten.

Wanda E. Santiago-Citron,
Deerfield, Wisconsin

Supplies: Image-editing software (Microsoft Digital Image Pro 10)

CHEESE BALL ADDICT

Renee's "crime scene" layout highlights her son's helpless love of cheese balls. Tear dark brown cardstock and adhere to light brown cardstock background. Print journaling onto ledger paper, trim, smudge edges with tea dye distress ink and layer with torn cardstock. Embellish with photo turns and black brads. Mat photo onto black cardstock. Affix title stickers to top of page. Print "headline" onto strip of paper and adhere; embellish with photo turns and black brads. Affix round letter stickers to small round tags and attach. Print quote onto ledger paper and smudge edges with tea dye distress ink. Smudge inside and outside of small file folder with tea dye distress ink. Mat photo on black cardstock and attach to inside of file folder. Mat second small photo onto black cardstock and attach to inside of file folder with hinges. Print "notes" on ledger paper and adhere to inside of file folder. Adhere hand photo to outside of file folder and adhere preprinted transparency and black frame over photo. Mat a second preprinted transparency onto small square of cream cardstock. Attach to file folder with staples. Embellish with file tabs, clip and date stamp. Adhere file folder element to page.

Renee Foss, Seven Fields, Pennsylvania

Supplies: *Cardstock (Bazzill); ledger paper, photo turns (Making Memories); letter stickers (K & Company); round letter stickers, small round tags (EK Success); date stamp (Stockwell); "evidence" transparency, black clip, cream file tab (7 Gypsies); file folder (Rusty Pickle); adhesive hinges (Destination Scrapbook Designs); distress ink (Ranger); letter tabs (Autumn Leaves); staples; black frame*

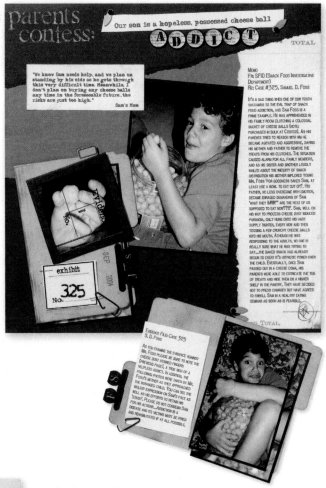

MY CAKE

Melissa makes "frosted" letters look good enough to eat on this page about her daughter's first baking experience. Double mat small rectangular photos onto pink, green and powder blue cardstocks, smudge with brown ink and adhere. Cut small photo squares. Mount one photo onto cardstock and smudge with brown ink. Adhere to small file folder. Adhere other photo to page. Cut large photo into half-circle and affix. Stamp words onto file folder tab. Scan Duncan Hines logo, print, trim and adhere to file folder. Affix mixing bowl, measuring spoons and measuring cup to file folder. Adhere file folder to page. Print journaling onto green cardstock and stamp word at bottom. Trim cardstock; smudge and ink edges with black ink. For title letters, fill in circles with colors and letters in word processing program. Print onto inkjet shrink paper and trim. Bake circles in oven; once circles begin to puff, remove and allow to cool. Rub tops with watermark ink, coat with extra thick embossing powder and heat emboss. Repeat process. Top final layer with small glass marbles.

Melissa Smith, North Richland Hills, Texas

Supplies: *Patterned paper, file folder (Rusty Pickle); shrink film (Grafix); letter stamps (Leave Memories); kitchen bowl embellishment (EK Success); small silver marbles (Willow Bead); extra thick embossing powder (Suze Weinberg); watermark ink (Tsukineko)*

I LOVE MY DOG

Heather used red cardstock to accent Kurtis' red swim trunks in this layout about a boy and his dog. Adhere top photos to patterned paper background with photo corners. Apply rub-on letters to page for title. Mat four small photos to red cardstock rectangle. Edge with chalk ink and attach to page. Affix alphabet stickers and embellish with black eyelets.

Heather Stanworth, Delta, Utah

Supplies: Patterned paper, stickers and letter stickers (Karen Foster Design); cardstock (Provo Craft); large rub-on letters (Doodlebug Design); letter/number stickers (Chatterbox); photo corners (3M); chalk ink (Clearsnap); eyelets; brown stamping ink

KALEB & CLYD

Greens and grays complement each other on Samuel's page about the bond between a boy and his dog. Edge light green cardstock background with black chalk. Cut strips of striped patterned paper and adhere to background. Splatter manila acrylic paint onto black cardstock and cut into two strips; adhere to page. Stamp title and dog bones onto black cardstock with color ink and adhere. Brush edges of photo with manila paint and affix over black cardstock below title. Adhere two short strips of splattered black cardstock onto green striped paper above title. Print journaling onto green cardstock, tear down one side, edge with black chalk and adhere; embellish with black brads. Punch four small holes into page below journaling and thread fiber in an "X" pattern. Stamp paw print onto dog tag charm, tie onto fiber and secure to page. Tear vellum quotes, edge with black chalk and adhere. Apply word sticker and handcut letters to create title. Embellish right side with black brads.

Samuel Cole, Stillwater, Minnesota

Supplies: Patterned paper (Hot Off The Press); cardstock (Bazzill); vellum preprinted quotes (Kopp Design); fibers (On The Surface); paw print, bone stamps (All Night Media, Stamp Craft); metal tag (Creative Impressions); acrylic paint (Making Memories); metal stamp pad (Hampton Art Stamps); alphabet letter (Hero Arts); chalk (Craf-T); brads; ink

FLUFFY LOVE

The loving relationship between a girl and her dog is illustrated in Melissa's Victorian-style layout. Mount patterned paper onto burgandy cardstock background. Print journaling onto transparency, trim, apply acrylic paint behind words and attach to page. Mount focal-point photo onto burgundy cardstock. Edge brown cardstock rectangle with brown ink and attach below photo. Print quote onto transparency and affix over brown cardstock. Edge thin strip of patterned paper and affix over transparency and photo. Embellish with metal photo corner. Edge small square photos and cardstock with ink; mount photos onto cardstock. Tie ribbon onto silver jewelry clasps and attach to back of photo mats. To create letter embellishments on small photos, press paper clay into jewelry blanks and stamp with letters. Paint with one coat of beige acrylic paint. Once dry, dab on red glass paint. Apply silver metallic rub-on letters onto raised impression areas of stamped images. Run wire through holes in jewelry blanks and attach behind photos. Create tassel accent with embroidery floss and attach to jewelry blank with wire. Adhere photos to page.

Melissa Smith, North Richland Hills, Texas

Supplies: *Patterned paper (Design Originals, K & Company); paper clay (Creative Paperclay Company); rubber stamps (Hampton Art Stamps); metallic rub-ons (Craf-T); jewelry clasps (Westrim); red glass paint (Delta); solvent ink (Tsukineko); jewelry blanks; silver beads; embroidery floss; wire; ribbon; metal photo corner (source unknown)*

FRIENDS FOREVER

Laura highlights the love between a little girl and her first kitten with red and natural tones. Cut a strip of blue patterned paper, edge with brown ink and affix to right side of page. Adhere photo to center of page. Print journaling onto strip of light cardstock, edge with brown ink and adhere to page below photo. Cut strips of red and white striped paper, edge with brown ink and affix to top and bottom of page, overlapping journaling block. Apply letter stamps to fabric tag and attach to molding with brad. Punch two rows of three small holes into top of page. Edge molding with brown ink and attach to top of page diagonally. Thread small pieces of fabric through holes and knot. Edge other strip of molding and adhere to bottom of page. Swipe metal letters with brown solvent ink and attach to bottom left of photo.

*Laura O'Donnell,
West Chester, Pennsylvania*

Supplies: *Patterned paper (Magenta, Melissa Frances); moldings (Chatterbox); ribbon, fabric tag (ScrapGoods); brad, metal words, date stamp (Making Memories); rubber stamps (Stampin' Up!); brown solvent ink (Tsukineko); cardstock*

OUR CHILDREN

Colorful chipboard letters tie Jane's clean-looking layout all together. Mat white cardstock onto black cardstocks. Double mat photo with brown and black cardstock background. Adhere to page. Adhere small brad letters and chipboard monograms around photo to create title. Apply rub-on date.

Jane F. Ecker, Batavia, New York

Supplies: Black cardstock (The Paper Company); white cardstock (Canson); brads (Provo Craft); chipboard monograms (Li'l Davis Designs); rub-on date (Creative Imaginations)

BROTHERS

Armed only with her computer and a beautiful photo of her sons, Rachel crafted all the crisp masculine page elements to contrast with the sweet boyish photo. Create border by cropping and layering side "paper." To achieve the gray colors, highlight a section of the border and change the Hue/Saturation. Use a pattern overlay to create main papers. Add a crinkle paper overlay for depth. Crop a rectangle out of the overlay, add a drop shadow and inner glow. Create bottle caps in drawing software and place in the square. Add the ribbon and title lettering with a drop shadow for each. Change the photo to feature sepia tones by manipulating the Hue/Saturation. Add a soft focus filter for a dreamy look. Apply a drop shadow. Add a tag to "hold" the photo. Include the date on the tag.

Rachel Dickson, Calgary, Alberta, Canada

Supplies: Image-editing software (Adobe Photoshop CS)

COMPLETE FLIRT

Jill created a feminine page using a combination of pretty pink and greens. Trim strip of green cardstock and attach to page. Layer and adhere printed vellums to right side of page. Adhere black cardstock rectangle on top of printed vellum. Cut preprinted transparency and affix to page in top right corner over black rectangle and in bottom left corner. Adhere rectangular piece of transparency to top left corner. Double mat photo, attach antique white photo turns to top and adhere over printed vellum. Attach green letter button to round tag. Tie green gingham ribbon and affix to page with foam adhesive. Affix word label onto small rectangle of striped paper. Mount onto small piece of printed black paper and then both onto small piece of black dotted cardstock. Mount all onto printed vellum. Attach black garters and adhere to page, securing garters on backside of page. Affix chipboard letters next to photo. Brush white paint onto metal molding strip. Once dry, attach to page over green cardstock strip. Tie green gingham ribbon onto metal message strip and attach on top of patterned metal strip. Adhere black buttons to bottom of page.

Jill Jackson-Mills, Roswell, Georgia

Supplies: *Patterned paper (EK Success); black cardstock (Bazzill); vellum (EK Success, NRN Designs); black garter (7 Gypsies); antique white photo anchors (Memories); metal flower clip (Eco Africa); woven label, molding strip (Making Memories); metal tag (K & Company); ribbon (Textured Trio); green gingham ribbon (Offray); black and white chipboard (Li'l Davis Designs); "love" frame (Daisy D's); black and white diamond frame (My Mind's Eye); black buttons; foam adhesive*

MY GREATEST LOVE

The blues in Toni's layout work in harmony with the black-and-white photo. Edge dark blue rectangle with brown chalk ink and adhere to page. Cut a large circle from lighter blue cardstock, edge half with brown chalk ink and lightly brush other half with white acrylic paint. Adhere to page over rectangle, trimming edges to be flush with edges of page. Edge dark blue square with brown chalk ink and embellish with decorative brad and painted silk flower. Adhere light blue rectangle to lower left corner of page. Cut two smaller circles from darker blue cardstock, edge with brown ink and affix over blue rectangle. Cut a small square from light blue cardstock and adhere in bottom left corner. Edge smaller light blue rectangle with brown ink and adhere to page. Affix thin strips of black cardstock to page. Stamp in two corners with acrylic paint. Crimp a piece of cardstock, brush with white and light blue acrylic paint and adhere to page. Print journaling onto vellum, cut into a square, edge with brown ink and affix to page. Mount photo onto black cardstock square and attach over vellum with hinges. Use black stamping ink and letter stickers to create title. Stamp remainder of title onto white cardstock with black acrylic paint. Cut and adhere to page, overlapping crimped cardstock. Embellish with silver heart brad.

Toni Holoubek, Rockford, Illinois

Supplies: *Foam stamps, brads (Making Memories); letter stickers (Creative Imaginations); silver heart brads (Provo Craft); chalk inkpad, hinges (Karen Foster Design); cardstock; acrylic paint*

SISTERS

The pastel colors in the photo carry over onto Johanna's soft layout about two sisters. Brush top and bottom edges of cardstock with lavender paint. Crumple patterned paper squares, tear, curl edges and adhere. Tear edge of green patterned paper, curl torn edge and adhere. Affix pink and purple ribbon down and across seams of page. Stitch through middle and around all edges of page. Adhere photo and frame with ribbon. Attach silk flowers around ribbon frame with painted brads. Add brads and safety pins with messages to corners. Print quote onto patterned paper strip, edge with brown chalk ink and embellish with ribbon and flower sticker. Sew to right side of page and embellish with brads. Edge small tags with brown chalk ink, embellish with ribbons and safety pin with message and adhere. Stamp titles across tags. Edge smaller photo with white acrylic paint and mount onto pink cardstock square. Stitch around edges, adhere to page and embellish with decorative brads. For title, apply rub-on letters and stamp with acrylic paints. Once dry, affix die cut letters on top. Paint oval frame with white acrylic paint. Once dry, embellish with ribbons, tie on small photo charms and adhere to page.

Johanna Peterson, El Cajon, California

Supplies: *Patterned paper (Daisy D's); cardstock (Bazzill); jewelry tags, die-cut letters, tag reinforcers (QuicKutz); letter stamps (PSX Design; magnetic stamps, paint, ribbon, oval frame, rub-on letters, decorative brads, foam stamps, safety pins, flowers (Making Memories); charm frames (7 Gypsies); mini brads (American Tag Co.); chalk ink (Clearsnap; ribbon (Offray); silk flowers; tags; pressed flower (artist's own)*

BROTHERS

This layout of greens, blues and browns perfectly complements the shirts Toni's boys are wearing. Spritz tan cardstock with green colorwash. Use strips of colorwashed cardstock and patterned papers to form background. Create a collage using printed die cuts and cut-outs from patterned paper. Mount photo onto spattered cardstock and affix to page. Embellish with file tab. Adhere bottom photo directly onto quote paper.

Toni Boucha, Spring, Texas

Supplies: *Patterned paper, all embellishments (KI Memories); green alcohol ink (Ranger); clear transparency; cardstock*

COUSINS

The simplicity of Samuel's layout allows the photo to be the focal point of the page. Trim and mount brown cardstock onto patterned paper frame. Tear patterned paper and adhere to brown cardstock. Thread fiber through costal netting, tie into a bow and adhere. Affix copper strip to page. Color pewter corner stickers and affix to corners of page. Mount photo onto patterned paper, and adhere to page over netting and copper. Print journaling and names onto tan paper and cut into three strips. Edge journaling strips with marker, mount onto cardstock strips and adhere to page. Stamp title onto tan cardstock and cut into geometric shapes. Affix to page using foam adhesive. Embellish page with decorative nailheads, tying twine "loops" around bottom three and affixing on back of page.

Samuel Cole, Stillwater, Minnesota

Supplies: Patterned paper (K & Company, Li'l Davis Designs, Magenta, Penny Black); brown cardstock (Bazzill); pewter corner stickers (Magenta); costal netting (Jest Charming Embellishments); copper sheet foil, rubber stamp, color brush twin marker (EK Success); solvent black inkpad (Tsukineko); twine; nailheads; foam adhesive

100% BEST FRIENDS

Melyssa's layout highlights the fun her son, Koale, and his cousins have together. Create background in image-editing software, using drop shadows to define the paper's edges. Open photos in image-editing software, crop and size. Place the focal photo over a brown mat and move to the left side. Add filmstrip images and place photos into them. Create text for title and journaling. Embellish by adding a clip, percent tag and staples.

Melyssa Connolly, Truro, Nova Scotia, Canada

Supplies: Image-editing software (Adobe Photoshop 7); All Boy page kit (www.scrapoutsidethebox.com)

LAUGH

I can't think of anything better than the sound of a child laughing. Especially a child who doesn't usually belly laugh like this! Tevin is one of those kids who, at least at family functions, tends to be kind of quiet and keep to himself. He's ten now—the age where he probably would rather be anywhere but in a house full of relatives! But Tevin is such a good kid. It encourages me to see a ten-year-old boy growing up in our society and turning out like Tevin. Happy. Funny. Well-adjusted. But mostly—sweet. Tevin is a sweet kid. He's always hugging us and he's always so polite. So when I capture this expression on film, I have to smile. He was telling us a story about Chad—a story that brought back a lot of memories of what it was like to have my brother around all the time! Tevin, I hope you continue to belly laugh—out loud and all the time!   [Age Ten * March * 2005]

out loud

Is that giggles I hear? No one can argue that a child's laughter can breathe life into an adult's otherwise monotonous day. We delight in their sweet giggles and sunny smiles. We take joy in their boisterous spirit and spunky personalities. Whether they're telling funny jokes, making silly faces or just being goofy all-around, kids keep us in stitches with their laughter. Of course, their personalities are not always upbeat and exuberant. They can also be grumpy, mischievous, melancholy or downright feisty. But if laughter is the best medicine then even the most cantankerous kid can bounce back with a good dose of the chuckles. All they need to do is to watch a funny movie, play with a beloved pet or read a book of comic strips, and their playful personalities come to life. So go ahead—laugh till your stomach hurts! Nothing will tickle you pink more than the glee and delight that echoes in a child's laughter.

CHAPTER THREE

SMILEY PUNKS

With darling "mugs" like these, Shannon couldn't resist creating a layout with a 1980s feel, complete with grunge letters, smashed bottle caps and safety pins. Adhere strips of graphic papers over black cardstock. Use ribbon to border the top and bottom of page. Print black-and-white photo and highlight boys with black pen squiggles. Add title and date stickers. Flatten bottlecaps with a hammer and poke a hole in the center of each with a screwdriver. Link three bottle caps together with safety pins and apply to page. In the opposite corner, adhere a bottle cap with a safety pin. Fasten remaining safety pins and apply the sticker label.

Shannon Taylor, Bristol, Tennessee

Supplies: Patterned papers, letter stickers and bottle caps (Mustard Moon); ribbon (Rusty Pickle); label maker (Dymo); black cardstock; safety pins; black pen

PLAY IS THE WORK OF CHILDHOOD

Mary used a combination of different textures to create a playful mood on her page. Ink edges of patterned cardstock background. Stitch across top and bottom of color blocks. Adhere photo to page and embellish with brads and photo turns. Use a variety of media to create title, inlcuding metal letters, letter stickers, rub-on letters, buttons, metal accents, letter stamps, die-cut letters, letter stencils and bottlecap. Add black label with name, season and year. Include inked tag with gingham ribbon for additional embellishment.

Mary MacAskill, Calgary, Alberta, Canada

Supplies: Patterned paper (Autumn Leaves, Scenic Route Paper Co.); photo turns, gold brads, bottle cap, alphabet stamps, button, ribbon (www.scraptivity.com); printed letter brad (Colorbök); cardstock tag, gold eyelet, metal letter, letter tile sticker (Making Memories); letter sticker, extreme eyelets, bolt (Creative Imaginations); shipping tag (Avery); stencil letters (Headline); rub-on letters; label maker (Dymo)

Photo Shoot Routine

Krista's layout perfectly showcases her daughter's "real" smile. Affix strips of polka-dot and red patterned papers to pink cardstock background. Adhere photos and embellish bottom photo with brads and silk flowers. Write title in small square of red paper and adhere to page. Print journaling onto white cardstock, cut words apart and affix to page, outlining random words with black pen. Embellish one word with page pebble. Write name and date in lower left corner.

Krista Fernendez, Fremont, California

Supplies: Patterned paper (Carolee's Creations); cardstock (Bazzill); brads, page pebble (Making Memories); black pen; silk flowers

Delight

Nicki used blue patterned papers to emulate the peace and tranquility of the ocean on this page about a walk on the beach. Tear blue patterned papers into pieces, edge with blue chalk and adhere to blue cardstock background. Sand edges of photos and affix to page. Smudge letter stencil with blue chalk, back with patterned paper and attach to page. Embellish with painted spiral clip. Smudge definition with blue chalk and affix to page. Print journaling onto cardstock, tear around the edges and adhere to page. Attach metal word to bottom left corner of page. Apply rub-on letters to page.

Nicki Foggin, Belleview, West Virginia

Supplies: Patterned paper (DieCuts with a View); cardstock (Bazzill, Worldwin); definition, rub-on letters, metal word (Making Memories); stencil (Headline); spiral clip; chalk

LAUGHING EYES

By stamping images onto patterned papers, Amy created personalized pattern papers which she used for her color-blocked background. Stamp script in brown ink over all papers. For left page, impress flower onto cream paper using green ink. Trim papers and adhere to background. Print quote in a circle and cut out. Ink edges and adhere to page. Add die-cut circles, rub-on letters and conchos. Mount focal photo, large sticker letters, glass photo corners and wood letters. For right page, create monogram letter by printing in reverse, cutting out and adding a brown mat. Create two cardstock matchbook-style covers. Close covers and stamp with medallion image. Add journaling block and photo inside each. Adhere to page. Apply rub-on letters between matchbooks and adhere label holder to frame the word.

Amy Goldstein, Kent Lakes, New York

Supplies: *Patterned papers (NRN Designs, SEI); letter stickers (American Crafts); rub-on letters (Making Memories, Scrapworks); large conchos (Scrapworks); wood letters (Li'l Davis Designs); glass photo corners (Stampington & Co.); polka-dot ribbon (Offray); stamping ink (Clearsnap); foam medallion stamp (Making Memories); flower stamp (Inkadinkado); text stamp (Hero Arts); metal label holder (Creative Imaginations); pink cardstock; green brads*

LAUGHTER

Nicole created visual interest by adding a fold-out element to her layout. Add camel ink to edges of cream cardstock. Adhere cream cardstock onto white cardstock background. Affix two hinges to left hand side of beige cardstock. Mat photo on peach cardstock and affix over hinges. For front of flap, mat another photo on peach cardstock and attach to hinges; add patterned paper and journaling printed on transparency to the back. Embellish flap with twill ribbon threaded through jump ring. Adhere strip of camel cardstock to bottom of layout. Cut stencil letters affixed over patterned paper and adhere to camel strip. Stamp descriptive words vertically on right side of cream cardstock. Stamp date and name on two pieces of peach cardstock. Staple one to bottom piece of peach cardstock; staple the other to top flap.

Nicole Cholet, Beaconsfield, Quebec, Canada

Supplies: *Patterned paper (KI Memories); hinges, staples (Making Memories); rubber stamps (EK Success); chalk (Craf-T); quote (www.two peasinabucket.com); embossing powder; cardstock; transparency; ink*

IMAGINE

A mother's devotion to her son is expressed in Alison's soft, sweet layout. Cut strips of various patterned papers and affix to white cardstock page. Mat photo onto patterned paper. Cut a half circle out of vellum and attach to page with flower brads. Print journaling onto blue patterned paper, write date at the bottom, trim and adhere to photo. Punch a hole in the top of flower die cut and tie on ribbon with word charm; attach to page.

*Alison Marquis,
Pleasant Grove, Utah*

Supplies: *Patterned paper, vellum (SEI); cardstock (Bazzill); mini flower brads (Making Memories); acrylic word "imagine" (Doodlebug Design); ribbon (Offray)*

LITTLE BOYS

Suzanne used a simple design to let the focus of her layout rest on the photo. Mat white cardstock onto green cardstock background. Attach fabric strip on right side. Stamp square in bottom left corner with acrylic paint. Adhere photo to page. Apply rub-on letters for title at top of page. Affix blue square stickers to top and bottom of page. Attach word pebble onto stamped square. Stamp date at bottom of page.

Suzanne Fisk, Grove City, Ohio

Supplies: Stickers, rub-on letters, date stamp (Making Memories); swatch, buttons (Junkitz); block stamp (Hero Arts); black ink; acrylic paint

SMILE

A variety of patterned papers creates an upbeat mood on Suzy's page. Adhere patterned paper section with rounded corners to red cardstock background. Affix die-cut letters to top of page for title. Print quote onto transparency and attach to page over title. Adhere photo to center of page. Attach pair of eyelets to page and thread with ribbon. Tie into a bow at top. Use letter stickers and blue pen for additional words.

Suzy West, Fremont, California

Supplies: Patterned paper (SEI); letter stencils (Pebbles); stickers (KI Memories); ribbon (Offray); cardstock; eyelets; blue pen

GIRLS

The patterned papers and colors on Leah's page work together to create feminine appeal. Ink patterned paper rectangles. Stitch papers to corners of blue cardstock background. Edge a small strip of green paper with ink and affix to page. Adhere black-and-white photo to page with green strip at top. Adhere lace over seam. Stamp journaling onto bottom rectangle and embellish with mini puzzle pieces and brads. Edge letter tabs with ink and smudge inside with green chalk. Attach to page and adhere photo on top with tabs sticking out on left side. Edge faux vintage label with ink, add lace, attach hangers to back and adhere to page. Affix wooden numbers between photos. Edge wooden letter tag with ink and embellish with fabric scrap.

Leah LaMontagne, Las Vegas, Nevada

Supplies: *Patterned paper (Amscan, Creative Imaginations, K & Company); wooden numbers (Li'l Davis Designs); wooden letter tag (Lara's Crafts); letter tabs (Autumn Leaves); rub-on letters (Making Memories); mini puzzle pieces (Limited Edition Rubberstamps); alphabet rubber stamps (Hero Arts); frame hangers (found at local hardware store); vintage tag (Melissa Frances); machine stitching, lace; stamping ink*

SIERRA SMILES

Suzy used primary colors to bring out the colors of her daughter's dress on this page. Edge patterned paper strips with brown ink and adhere to blue cardstock background. Smudge rickrack with ink and affix to page. Attach metal word charm. Print quote onto white cardstock and attach to page. Mount photo onto white cardstock using photo corners; adhere to red paper at an angle. Attach clear file tab to side of photo and affix label on top. Adhere ribbon to bottom of page and embellish with silk flower. Edge small white cardstock pieces with ink and adhere to right side of page. Affix label to right side of page. Edge entire page with brown ink.

Suzy West, Fremont, California

Supplies: *Patterned paper (KI Memories); cardstock (Bazzill); flowers (Michaels); photo corners (Chatterbox); rickrack (Jo-Ann Stores); label maker (Dymo); ribbon; index tab*

IN THE MOUTH

Amy's retro page features 1960s colors, graphic papers and round corners for a fun and funky look. Print journaling on large dot paper. Print title on tan cardstock. Using brown ink, stamp medallion onto pink cardstock. Trim all papers and round corners with a corner punch. Adhere papers to background. Mount photo. Add handcut flower to a metal-rimmed tag, adhering with a brad at the center.

Amy Goldstein, Kent Lakes, New York

Supplies: *Patterned papers (American Crafts, Scrapworks); corner rounder punch (Marvy); metal-rimmed tag, foam medallion stamp (Making Memories); brown stamping ink; pink, tan and brown cardstocks*

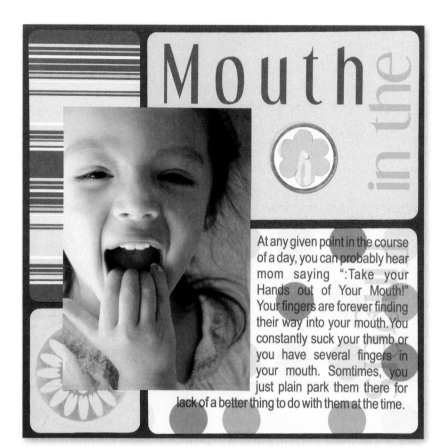

At any given point in the course of a day, you can probably hear mom saying ":Take your Hands out of Your Mouth!" Your fingers are forever finding their way into your mouth. You constantly suck your thumb or you have several fingers in your mouth. Somtimes, you just plain park them there for lack of a better thing to do with them at the time.

HE IS ALREADY HER HERO

Heather's layout focuses on the relationship between a little girl and her big brother. Adhere striped strip of paper to patterned paper background. Stamp and apply rub-on letters to create title. Adhere photos to page and embellish with rub-on letters, stickers and heart brad. Affix stickers to small label. Punch one small hole on each side and thread string through. Affix on back of page with tape.

Heather Stanworth, Delta, Utah

Supplies: *Patterned paper (Darby); address alphabet stickers, word stickers, label (Chatterbox); string, rub-on letters (Making Memories); alphabet stamps (Ma Vinci's Reliquary); heart brad (DecoArt); black ink*

SILLY BOYS

Graphic papers, paint smudges and two silly subjects all work together for a jovial effect on Colleen's layout. Trim patterned paper into strips and blocks. Layer paper, smudging edges with black paint before adhering. Double mat photo and add to page. Stamp title using black paint. Create a page embellishment using a tag, fabric label, skeleton leaves and a sticker word. Print journaling onto white paper and tuck inside a file folder. Add a matted block to the front. Wrap a ribbon around the file folder and both ends of a buckle; secure with brads. Add a paper clip to top right edge of folder. Apply label words to file folder.

Colleen Stearns, Natrona Heights, Pennsylvania

Supplies: Patterned papers (Chatterbox); foam letter stamps, sticker (Making Memories); paper clip (EK Success); gingham ribbon (May Arts); fabric label (Me & My Big Ideas); tag (Rusty Pickle); skeleton leaves (Graphic Products Corp.); label maker (Dymo); file folder (Rusty Pickle); black solvent ink (Tsukineko); green brads; putty, gray and celery cardstocks; buckle; twine; black acrylic paint

Oh, how silly my boys tend to get at times! The littlest thing can send them into a fit of giggles, and once that starts- look out!- the goofiness begins! Jacob usually sets everything off by making a funny face or a strange noise, and then Ian joins in, mimicking his older brother. Soon, they are dancing around, arms waving, legs kicking and laughter resonating. Faces red from laughter, they eventually collapse on the floor, exhausted from the hard work of kids' play. This summer day in 2003 was no different. JC and I took the boys to burn off some energy at Deer Lakes Park. They abandoned the bikes they were riding and started chasing each other. Before long, the "tag, you're it" evolved into tickles and fits of laughter. I love moments like these! I hope Jacob and Ian will always be able to let go a little and be silly.

KRYSTAL

A greeting card was the inspiration behind Sherrill's very girly page. Tear strips of patterned paper and cardstock. Edge with ink and embossing powder and adhere to patterned paper background. Embellish page with stamps and shapes embossed with gold embossing powder. Tear white cardstock and mat photo; adhere to page. Adhere other photo in top right corner. Stamp heart onto large square metal-rimmed tag and heat emboss. Attach to page under center photo. Affix specialty paper to page in upper left corner and letter stickers at bottom.

Sherrill Ghilardi Pierre, Maplewood, Minnesota

Supplies: Patterned paper (KI Memories); letter stickers (Doodlebug Design); extra thick embossing powder (Suze Weinberg); flower rubber stamp, leaf rubber stamp (Close To My Heart); words rubber stamp (Hero Arts); metal-rimmed tag (Making Memories); specialty paper; pink ink; embossing powder

PICTURE DAY

Jenn used conversation journaling to tell the story behind her son's silly facial expressions. Print title on dark gray cardstock and adhere to light gray cardstock background. Print journaling on transparency using blue ink and attach to page. Trim and layer strips of navy blue and dark gray cardstocks, dark blue ribbon and silver mesh. Crop and adhere photos to layout. Use embroidery floss to secure button embellishments to strips of cardstock.

Jenn Brookover, San Antonio, Texas

Supplies: *Cardstock (Bazzill, Doodlebug Design); mesh (Creative Imaginations); ribbon (Making Memories); buttons; floss; transparency*

CRAZY YOU

Bright colors make the black-and-white photo on Erin's page really stand out, and the variety of patterned papers creates a "crazed" feeling. Create a "crazy quilt" background pattern using strips of different patterned papers. Write on tab, attach to photo and adhere to page. Affix letter stickers to bottom of page.

Erin Sweeney, Twinsburg, Ohio

Supplies: *Patterned paper, tab (KI Memories); letter stickers (American Crafts); black pen*

EVEN A PRINCESS

In creating this layout, Suzy knew that being 6 is about being silly, even when you're a princess. Cut a strip of patterned paper and adhere to left side of background. Print journaling on transparency, trim and adhere over strip. Using small circles paper, cut a "C" shaped frame, rounding corners. Mat photo onto striped paper with round corners and adhere over patterned strip and blue background. Punch holes through layers down left side of striped mat and along inside of circles frame. Tie ribbons through pairs of holes. Create title using a mixture of stickers, metal, wood and rub-on letters. Apply clear acrylic sealer to sticker and wood letters. Trim oval from pink paper and embellish with silk daisy and rhinestones. Adhere additional rhinestones to ribbon, letters and papers.

Suzy West, Fremont, California

Supplies: Patterned papers and die cuts (KI Memories); corner rounder (Marvy); rub-on letters, enamel letters (Making Memories); metal letters (Colorbök); letters (Li'l Davis Designs); letter stickers (American Crafts); rhinestones (Michaels); acrylic sealer (Ranger); transparency; silk daisy; ribbons

BROTHERS

Shannon used a transparency overlay to share the unique friendship that grows between brothers. Crop photo and adhere over patterned paper background. Trim and chalk edges of two strips of beige cardstock. Adhere strips of cardstock to desired places on background. Place transparency overlay onto layout and adhere at corners. Adhere canvas tag to right side of layout; secure with large eyelet. Add additional eyelets along the right edge and embellish with jump rings and charm. Trim another piece of beige cardstock, ink edges and stamp journaling. Adhere cardstock over canvas tag and part of transparency. Add walnut ink tag embellished with eyelet and jump ring. Use letter stamps and rub-on letters to create title on walnut ink and canvas tags.

Shannon Taylor, Bristol, Tennessee

Supplies: Patterned paper, cardstock, walnut ink tag and canvas tag (Rusty Pickle); transparency (Artistic Expressions); rub-on letters (Making Memories); letter stamps (Hero Arts); jump rings (Junkitz); eyelets; chalk

A Tale of Two Brothers

Sande's patchwork of color and phrases work together to emphasize the sometimes silly relationship between two brothers. Adhere patterned paper to left side of patterned cardstock background. Stitch twill and small pieces of patterned paper to cardstock. Print journaling onto green and lavender cardstock, cut apart into small rectangles and attach to page with staples. Attach brads, conchos and large letters to page for title.

Sande Krieger, Salt Lake City, Utah
Photo: Jessie Stringham Photography,
West Jordan, Utah

Supplies: Patterned paper (KI Memories, Scenic Route Paper Co.); twill (Scenic Route Paper Co.); quote paper (KI Memories); metal alphabet, staples (Making Memories); round metal letters (Jo-Ann Stores)

Say Cheese

The pink used in Sonya's layout really works to make the black-and-white photos stand out. Edge patterned papers with distress ink and adhere to white cardstock background. Adhere three small photos to left side of page. Trim block of vellum and punch hole. Ink edges of block and hole and attach vellum to page over photos with brads. Smudge white cardstock with distress ink. Mount focal-point photo onto cardstock and adhere to page. Stamp portion of title onto pink cardstock rectangles edged with ink and adhere to page. Print remainder of title onto transparency, cut into strip and attach to page with brads. Affix quote stickers to page and edge entire page with ink.

Sonya Russell, Fortson, Georgia

Supplies: Patterned paper, sticker quotes (Imagination Project); cardstock (Bazzill); snaps (Making Memories); rubber stamps (Li'l Davis Designs); distressed ink (Ranger); ink; vellum; transparency

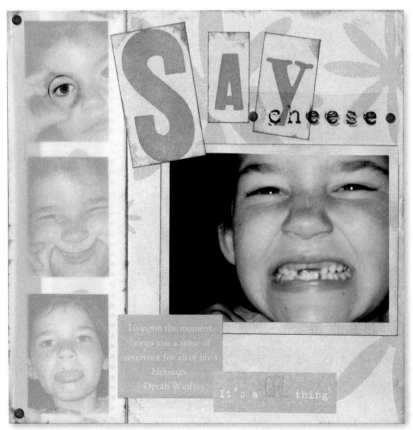

APPLE ORCHARD

Christine used blues and greens to add dimension to a layout about picking apples. Crumple patterned paper, flatten and smudge with brown ink. Curl edges and adhere to green cardstock. Tear strips of blue paper. Ink edges and adhere to top and bottom of page. Crumple red paper, flatten and cut two strips. Attach to top and bottom of page with brads. Mat large photo on red cardstock and adhere. Mount medium and small photos on green cardstock tags and adhere to page with brads. Embellish medium photo with round plastic letter buttons. Print journaling onto smudged green paper. Mount onto smudged blue paper and affix to page. Print title onto green cardstock and cut apart. Attach to page with silver eyelets and embellish with raffia. Attach letter eyelets to bottom of page to finish title. Embellish page with ribbon and apple buttons tied with raffia.

Christine Brown, Hanover, Minnesota

Supplies: Patterned paper (Paper Adventures); ribbon (Michaels); buttons (Hirschberg, Schutz & Co., Junkitz); snaps (Making Memories); raffia; cardstock

I LOVE ALL YOUR MANY FACES

On this page, Heather used many different patterns to express "many faces." Layer torn paisley patterned paper with inked edges and block of polka-dot vellum to patterned paper background. Crumple, flatten, tear, smudge and edge light blue paper. Adhere to page and embellish with green brads. Attach frames with cream brads. Affix letter stickers inside frames to spell portion of title. Stamp remainder of title onto blue paper. Adhere photos to page. Affix word stickers to corners of photos and letter and number stickers to bottom of page. Fold over top left corner and secure with brad.

Heather Stanworth, Delta, Utah

Supplies: Patterned paper, vellum, frames, tacks, letter stickers (Chatterbox); chalk ink (Clearsnap)

MOODY BLUES

Mac emphasized the many moods of a teenager with blues and greens in this layout. Layer and adhere patterned papers, green cardstock shapes and torn blue cardstock with inked edges onto dark green cardstock background. Doublemat focal-point photo with green and blue cardstocks, fold edge of cardstock over photo, punch holes and tie ribbons to left side. Adhere smaller photo and create frames from patterned paper and green cardstock edged with ink; embellish with word pebble. Cut trapezoids from patterned papers and ink edges. Affix letter stickers for portion of title, mount all together and adhere to page. Use jelly jar dipped in green acrylic paint to add circles and foam stamps dipped in blue acrylic paint to add remainder of title. Print journaling on blue cardstock, tear and ink edges and affix over patterned paper rectangle; embellish with sticker, ribbon and eyelet. Create journaling pocket by stitching inked cardstock and patterned paper trapezoids. Paint letter stencil and affix to front of pocket; adhere element to page. Embellish page with brown ribbon, metal flower with green eyelet, and stickers. Affix cardstock word stickers to bottom right corner and frame with large square brads.

Mac L. Stanley, Conway, Arkansas

Supplies: Patterned paper (KI Memories, Scrapworks); cardstock (Bazzill); die cuts (Scrapworks); stickers (EK Success); rub-on letters, letter stickers, foam stamps (Making Memories); distress ink (Ranger); ribbon (Offray); letter stencil

EMOTIONS RUN WILD AT THE ZOO

Renee features how Sam's emotions run the gamut on this page about a trip to the zoo. Print journaling onto tan cardstock background. Mount photos onto brown cardstock and adhere. Affix definition stickers to photos. Use letter stamps and chipboard letters to create title. Adhere tiger photo to page, tie ribbon around metal frame and attach over photo. Embellish animal pictures with eyelets and adhere to bottom of page.

Renee Foss, Seven Fields, Pennsylvania

Supplies: Patterned paper, stickers, brad, eyelets, chalk (Pebbles); frame, ribbon, magnetic alphabet stamp, definition stickers (Making Memories); black solvent ink (Tsukineko); chalk ink (Clearsnap); letter stickers (Creative Imaginations); dimensional adhesive (Ranger); chipboard rectangles (Bazzill)

CAPRICIOUS

Michaela used pink and blue to create an eye-catching page about Catalina's many moods. Print journaling onto pink cardstock background. Adhere blue cardstock rectangles and photos to page. Print adjectives onto vellum, cut into small squares and adhere. Attach blue frames with small silver eyelets over vellum and connect with jump rings. Write name onto small vellum square and adhere. Attach blue frame with small silver eyelets and embellish with heat-embossed die-cut letter. Attach photo turns to page with brads. Trim vellum hearts and blue die-cut letter "J" to create dragonfly embellishments. Embellish hearts with silver embossing powder and adhere to page.

Michaela Young-Mitchell,
Morenci, Arizona

Supplies: *Cardstock (Bazzill); photo turns (7 Gypsies); mini brads (Karen Foster Design); die-cut shapes, slide mount, heart (QuicKutz); heart stamp (source unknown); pen; embossing powder*

GIGGLY, PLAYFUL SIERRA

Suzy incorporated simple, soft pinks into her layout to complement this photo of one of Sierra's many moods. Adhere block of white paper to patterned paper background. Trim block of patterned paper, ink edges and adhere. Print journaling onto pink cardstock, trim, ink edges and adhere. Adhere photo to page with photo corners. Print adjectives onto pink cardstock, cut into rectangles and affix to white rectangles edged with ink. Adhere and embellish with small silver eyelets. Affix letters to create title and embellish with small silver eyelets. Attach pink ribbon to top and bottom of patterned paper block. Add silk flowers with pink brads.

Suzy West, Fremont, California

Supplies: *Patterned paper, letter tabs (Mustard Moon); ribbon, flowers (Michaels); mini eyelets, colored brads (Making Memories)*

MAGICALLY DELICIOUS

Shannon's St. Patrick's Day photo shoot turned for the better with the help of a green lollipop. Chalk green cardstock background. Trim large block of patterned paper and adhere. Trim page protector into a large block and a small square; crumple. Using green stained-glass spray, paint the backs. Once dry, cut out a four-leaf clover from small square and set aside; sew the large block over patterned paper. Trim two small pieces of green fabric, fold and stitch to opposite corners. Adhere rickrack border along bottom. Crop photos and mat onto green cardstock with chalked edges. Add a green eyelet to the lower edge of focal-point photo. Staple corners and mount onto page. Paint chipboard letter, attach to ball chain and connect to eyelet. Print journaling and title on green cardstock, trim, chalk edges and mount. Adhere clover cut-out to glass tag, thread rickrack through hole and adhere.

Shannon Taylor, Bristol, Tennessee

Supplies: Clover paper (Sonburn); green ball chain (Magic Scraps); chipboard letter and green staples (Making Memories); green fabric (Junkitz); stained-glass spray paint (Krylon); dimensional adhesive (JudiKins); glass tag; green cardstock; page protector; staples; rickrack; chalk; acrylic paint

magically delicious

SILLY, COOL, OLD GLASSES

A fun pair of old glasses is the subject of Marie's page. Mount photo onto lavender cardstock and adhere to cream cardstock background. Affix patterned paper strips and ribbon to right side of page. Smudge white tags with lavender chalk, affix stickers and attach to page with brads. Adhere large brown tag to bottom right of page and embellish with large silver brad. Affix painted jigsaw and handcut letters to tag.

Marie Cox, Springfield, Massachusetts

Supplies: Patterned paper (KI Memories); cardstock (Bazzill); ribbon (Michaels); transparency (Magic Scraps); tag (A. C. Moore); brads

ALL EARS

Becky's use of browns and blues in this page work together to perfectly complement this silly picture of Kristin. Print journaling onto speckled cardstock background and brush edges with acylic paint. Trim patterned paper and blue cardstock strip, brush edges and adhere. Embellish strip with conchos. Stamp title at top of page with acrylic paint and adhere epoxy letter stickers. Adhere photo to bottom of page.

Becky Thompson, Fruitland, Idaho

Supplies: Patterned paper (Karen Foster Design); epoxy letter stickers (Target); alphabet foam stamps, acrylic paint (Making Memories); nailheads (www.memoriesoftherabbit.com)

Listening? That's definitely one of your strengths, Kristin, and something I hope will carry with you through your life. It's a great skill to be a good listener, and it's not something everybody does well. You are blessed that it comes so naturally to you.

The saying goes that you only have one mouth, but two ears — because the emphasis is supposed to be on listening and not always speaking. Granted, you're a first-rate chatterbox, but if you can continue to know when to just be still and listen, then you'll be fine, and your friends and family will benefit from your ability to be a good listener.

I love you my girl – always remember that it's more important sometimes to just listen than to have anything to say. You never know who might need those listening ears of yours.
April 2003

TIME FOR A BIGGER BOX

Polly used pink and green with a dash of houndstooth check to coordinate perfectly with Lauren's outfit. Tear strip of pink patterned papers and adhere to green patterned paper background. Affix photos to page, tucking edges of left and right photos under paper strip. Mount middle photo onto patterned paper at an angle and embellish with ribbon. Stamp round metal-rimmed tag and embellish with clock charm. Thread onto wide ribbon, tie in a bow and adhere to top of page. Adhere additional ribbon with bow to bottom of page. Use stamps and letter brads to create title. Stamp name and date in lower left corner.

Polly McMillan, Bullhead City, Arizona

Supplies: Patterned paper (KI Memories); ribbon (Offray); clock charm (www.maudeandmillie.com); letter stamps (FontWerks, PSX Design); letter brads (Li'l Davis Designs)

BOYS

Gray and beige combined with vellum keep the tone of Nic's layout soft and uncluttered. Trim large blocks of patterned paper, light gray cardstock and clear vellum; ink edges. Print journaling on cardstock, trim into block and ink edges. Layer patterned paper, cardstock and vellum on gray cardstock background. Layer and adhere boy stickers in bottom left corner. Stamp title on vellum, ink edges and adhere over stickers. Trim strips of patterned paper, ink edges and adhere over vellum. Crop photos and apply white rub-on letters to add names. Trim additional pieces of cardstock, ink edges and mount photos; adhere to layout.

Nic Howard, Pukekone,
South Auckland, New Zealand

Supplies: Patterned paper, stickers (Rebekka Erickson); cardstock (Bazzill); stamps (Ma Vinci's Reliquary); rub-on letters (Making Memories); vellum; black stamping ink

SOMEDAY

Cori's pink layout highlights the relationship between two sisters in pink sweaters. Print journaling onto white cardstock rectangle. Mount photo onto pink cardstock and adhere to white rectangle. Affix to patterned paper background. Attach vellum strips to bottom of page with white brads. Adhere photos in between strips. Attach vellum strip to top of page with white brads and affix title stickers on top. Embellish with flower stickers.

Cori Dahmen, Vancouver, Washington

Supplies: Patterned paper, stickers (Doodlebug Design); vellum; eyelets; pen

Boys Are the Ultimate Adventure

To accent her title block, Heather created a tag by stamping into air-dry clay and embellishing it once dry. She also used colorwash ink to tint two photos. Roll out a thin layer of air-dry clay. Stamp a diamond pattern into it, trim edges and let dry. Using colorwash ink, paint entire piece of clay. Rub ink over raised diamonds. Embellish with stickers, fabric and photo corner. Using as little colorwash as possible on a makeup sponge, wipe inward from the edges of two photos. Adhere photos, cork and clay title to page. Stamp images around photos. Embellish page with metal elements.

Heather Stanworth, Delta, Utah

Supplies: Patterned paper (Pebbles); numbers strip stamp (Club Scrap); letter stamps (Ma Vinci's Reliquary); air-dry clay (Provo Craft); diamond patterned stamp (Impress Rubber Stamps); alcohol ink (Ranger); brown solvent ink (Tsukineko); letter stickers (Sticker Studio); fabric labels, photo hinges, metal photo corners, rub-on letters, photo turns (Making Memories); cork; brads; muslin; brown stamping ink

Raindrops

Shannon's photos make it look as though her son could leap off the page and drip all over your couch! Using software plug-ins, she designed the splattered paper mat on the right side. Open photos in image-editing software, crop and place on the canvas. Apply a filter to create the look of a watercolor. Create mat boxes for the photos, fill with color and feather edges for a softer look. Create text box and type title. Apply an inner shadow and outer glow. Add a bevel and embossed edge to the letters. Add brad and bar elements. Finish with journaling.

Shannon Taylor, Bristol, Tennessee

Supplies: Image-editing software (Adobe Photoshop, Alien Skin Software Eye Candy 4000)

FUN AND GAMES

Tricia echoed the chocolate-filled faces in her photos by adding smudges of white paint to patterned papers and brown stamping ink to premade tags. Smudge butter cream cardstock background with brown ink. Choose patterned papers and use sandpaper, ink and paint to distress. Trim papers to create a color-block collage on the background. Trim photos and mat on brick red paper. Add a second mat to the boys' photos. Turn top right corner down, trim and add a rivet. Print journaling block on butter cream cardstock and trim. Use ink to distress journaling and tags. Add letter stickers to create title. Embellish page with round and star snaps. Stamp date using black ink.

Tricia Rubens, Castle Rock, Colorado

Supplies: Patterned papers, round and star snaps, friendship tags and letter stickers (Chatterbox); date stamp (Making Memories); black and brown stamping ink; white acrylic paint; butter cream cardstock; rivet; sandpaper

GIRLY GIRLS

Thomisia's page highlights her girls' fashion show with coordinating papers and embellishments in hot pink, gray and black. For left page, using gray paper as the background, adhere a strip of words paper. Sand a block of hot pink paper and ink edges. Crop and mat focal-point photo onto gray cardstock; adhere over block. Adhere ribbon to upper right corner of photo; create flower embellishment with rhinestones and swirl button. Apply rub-on letters to photo. Crop and mat additional photos onto pink cardstock with inked edges; accent with swirl clips and letter conchos. For right page, using sanded hot pink paper as the background, adhere a strip of gray paper to left side. Add a strip of words paper. Crop and mat photos onto gray and pink cardstocks; embellish with heart button and swirl clip. Trim gray paper and pink circles to fit on tag. Embellish with ribbon, concho letters and die-cut letters.

Thomisia Francois, Duncanville, Texas

Supplies: Patterned papers (Basic Grey, DieCuts with a View); letter conchos (Colorbök); die-cut letters (Sizzix); black polka-dot ribbon (Textured Trio); heart button (source unknown); swirl button (Jesse James); rub-on letters; pink and gray cardstocks; black stamping ink; pink rhinestones; sandpaper; swirl paper clips

FRIENDS

Aimee trimmed soft-colored cardstocks into blocks for an endearing page featuring two siblings and their cousin. Begin by cutting pastel cardstocks into a variety of blocks and ink edges black. Mix colors and shapes and layer around patterned cardstock background. Using embroidery floss, sew on a variety of buttons. Apply rub-on letters and mount photo.

Aimee Grenier, Hinton, Alberta, Canada

Supplies: Patterned papers (source unknown); rub-on letters (Making Memories); buttons (Doodlebug Design); green, white, pink and yellow cardstocks (Bazzill); green, yellow and pink embroidery floss; black stamping ink

FRIENDS

Melissa surrounded a group of giggly girls with feminine and funky papers and recorded their names on a tag tucked behind the photo. Trim striped papers with inked edges to mat enlarged photo. Mount die-cut title letters to a premade tag and add journaling to another. Wipe the edges with black ink. Adhere photo mat to patterned paper background. Then use double-sided tape to create a pocket on the back of the photo to hold the journaling tag and keep it from sliding completely underneath. Adhere the photo and tuck the tag into pocket. Thread ends of self-adhesive rickrack through holes in the title tag and secure.

Melissa Ackerman, Princeton, New Jersey

Supplies: Patterned papers and tags (Basic Grey); die-cut letters (QuicKutz); self-adhesive rickrack (Colorbök); photo corner punch (EK Success); black cardstock; pink rickrack; black pen; black stamping ink

bookworm

Kendra is such a bookworm! Her nose is in a book all summer long. Some days she stays in her jammies all day, reading. She even re-reads some of her favorites when she runs out of new books. When asked to do something, her frequent refrain is, "Just one more page." Fortunately, I was the exact same way at her age, so even though I might get frustrated when there are chores to be done, or when I feel like she needs to get outside and enjoy the sunshine, I can relate to the gravitational pull of a good book.
Photo: Summer 2003
Journaling: Summer 2004

Kids are fascinated with exploration and learning. They love to pepper their parents and teachers with a mountain of questions. Why does a jaguar's eyes glow? Does a curveball really curve? Is it true that no two dogs have the exact same nose print? Kids find excitement in anything that will stir their imaginations and ignite discovery. A child can peer at the stars through an ordinary telescope and pretend to be seeing through the lens of the Hubble. A group of scouts can explore a trail map outlining the terrain of Rocky Mountain National Park to determine where to set up camp. A class of sixth graders can stand in awe as they observe the Egyptian exhibit of pyramids and sculptures at a local museum. So put on your thinking cap and embrace every experience that offers opportunity for your kids to be enlightened. Whether they're reading the latest *Harry Potter* novel, collecting insects and butterflies or studying other cultures and customs, kids will never cease to amaze us with their sense of wonder.

LITTLE BOOK WORM

Polly created this page highlighting her daughter's favorite books by writing titles neatly onto white paper and placing them in tiny metal frames. Stamp title word onto patterned paper and add sticker letters, tickets, buttons and ribbon. Mount onto patterned paper background. Add patterned paper strips to bottom and right side of page. Layer photo mats, angled photos, circle photo and ribbons. Trim white cardstock, handwrite book titles and adhere to page with frames. Stamp word onto small square of patterned cardstock, trim, add small decorative buttons and adhere to page. Add rickrack to top of page.

Polly McMillan, Bullhead City, Arizona

Supplies: Patterned papers (K & Company); black rickrack (Trim-Tex); letter stamps (PSX Design); letter stickers (American Crafts, Creative Imaginations); raffle ticket blanks (www.maudeandmillie.com); blue polka-dot ribbon (May Arts); mini frames (Jo-Ann Stores); ribbon (May Arts, Offray); cream and white cardstocks; buttons; rickrack; black pen

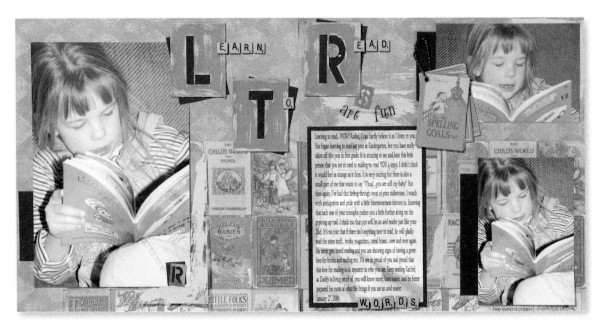

LEARN TO READ

Learning to read is one of life's greatest challenges and pleasures. Ginger created a tag book by cutting out collage paper books and backing some with reduced photos of her daughter reading. Trim book patterned paper and add to the bottom of the spread. Cut out books from another sheet of patterned paper and adhere the covers back to back. Mounting a few photos in place of covers. Punch a hole in the top left corner of each and thread onto ball chain. Cut transparency into several pieces. Paint swashes of blue and let dry. Add the transparency pieces to the layout. In image-editing software, open a photo, reduce the opacity and type journaling over the image. Size the photo to accommodate text, print and mat on black paper. Adhere black cardstock blocks, photos and book embellishment. Paint stencil letters; add to page with wood letters and metal stencil letter.

Ginger McSwain, Cary, North Carolina

Supplies: Patterned papers (Design Originals, K & Company); children's storybooks collage paper (Design Originals); stencil letters (Hunt); wooden title letters (Card Connection); metal stencil letters (Colorbök); letter stickers (Me & My Big Ideas); ball chain; star brad; black cardstock; blue acrylic paint; transparency

BORN READER, NOT

Echoing the colors of Cody's book cover, Dar created a simple yet dramatic page. For left page, trim strips of blue, black and green cardstocks, ink edges and adhere over green cardstock background. Print journaling onto white cardstock, trim and ink edges. Double mat photo and adhere. Affix letter stickers to create title. Apply rub-on letters to small tags on large jump ring. For right page, trim strips of blue, black and green cardstocks, ink edges and adhere to green cardstock background. Double mat photos. Affix letter stickers vertically.

Dar Kaso, Virginia Beach, Virginia

Supplies: Letter stickers (Doodlebug Design); jewelry tags (DMD); swirl paper clip (Boxer Scrapbook Productions); rub-on letters (Making Memories); black, white, blue, powder blue, avocado and spring green cardstocks; black stamping ink

I'M A MAIL SEEKER

Jill created this page documenting the daily ritual of her daughter bringing in the mail, often being disappointed that nothing arrives for her. Trim script paper, cut out rectangle from upper left corner and adhere to patterned paper background. Mat photos and mailbox stickers onto black cardstock. Adhere along with letter stickers, ribbon and chipboard letters.

Jill Jackson-Mills, Roswell, Georgia

Supplies: Patterned papers (7 Gypsies, Paper Loft); mailbox stickers (Mary Engelbreit); black letter stickers (Creative Imaginations); chipboard letters (Li'l Davis Designs); ribbon (Textured Trio); black cardstock

MISCHIEF

Dana modified the background of the photo of her son and his frog, making the image jump right off the page. Create a color-blocked background using three tones of blue cardstock, beginning with the lightest as the background. Trim blocks of medium and dark blues, ink edges and sew onto page. Open photo in image-editing software. Create a duplicate layer and decrease the hue/saturation levels to make the layer black-and-white. Use the eraser tool and erase the subject so that the color layer will show. Use the "smudge" tool to blur the background. Print photo, ink edges and mat onto burlap. Punch four holes in focal-point photo and burlap mat, and tie ribbons through holes. Hand sew photo turns onto burlap and mount on background. Ink edges of small photo and mat onto light blue, torn-edge block. Punch holes in mat and add ribbons. Adhere twill ribbon to page and stamp title word in brown ink. Adhere buttons, ribbons and journaling sticker to complete the page.

Dana Ramsey, Jacksonville, Florida

Supplies: Blue burlap (Paper Palette); ribbons (May Arts); boy twill (Creative Impressions); word stamp (Memories in the Making); phrase sticker and tag (Autumn Leaves); brown solvent ink (Tsukineko); photo turns (Making Memories); image-editing software (Adobe Photoshop Elements 2.0); brown buttons; blue cardstocks (Bazzill); black pen

LOOK WHAT I FOUND

Stacy's photos show her son's avid curiousity and her journaling describes his love for adventure. Cut strip of orange paper, distress with black and red stamping inks and adhere to left side of blue cardstock background using flathead eyelets. Embellish the journaling envelope using stamped images and inked edges. Adhere at an angle so the journaling block slides in easily. Mount photos on white cardstock and onto the page. Add an orange name tab to focal-point photo. Create title by reverse printing letters onto orange cardstock and cutting out. Mount the letters along the bottom right corner of the page and finish the title with block letter stickers. Add embellishments, including the date and label holder, the subject's initial and an epoxy sticker.

Stacy McFadden,
Doncaster East, Victoria, Australia

Supplies: Block letter stickers, clock stamp and checkerboard stamp (Collections Australia); label holder (source unknown); date stamp (Office Works); letter cut-out (Foofala); epoxy word sticker (source unknown); blue, orange, black and white cardstocks; metallic brads; black leather cord; craft paper envelope; black and white stamping inks; black pen

It's amazing what thrills a snail can give a couple of kids. Our home has gardens lined with Agapanthus. It is the perfect snail hideout. Jacob and Braden go on snail hunts and I guess the snails don't really have a chance. The boys are armed with empty vegemite jars. They stuff them full of grass they have pulled out of the lawn, Then they stalk the snails. They sneak up and push the agapanthus leaves apart and jump at the snails, as if the snails might run away and they need to catch them before they make their escape.

I have to remind the kids not to leave their snail jars in the sun. There is only so long a snail can live with 50 of his friends in the baking hot sun. I also have to remind them that snails don't like water. I was pretty upset to find a jar chocka full of snails once, and full to the brim with water. Yes Jacob, snails like to stay damp, but they can't swim. Sorry dude. No, they aren't just sleeping.

GOT YA

Slimy little dude

GOT YA

Nic combined monochromatic orange tones with graphic black-and-white papers to keep the focus on the boy and his snail. Begin with darker orange as the background. Trim vellum and adhere to page, leaving a border of orange at the top and bottom. Cut strips, rectangles and blocks from several striped papers to create matting and borders; adhere. Print journaling on peach cardstock, trim and apply rub-on letters to the bottom. Trim two long strips off the page and crop the center square. Ink edges and apply as shown. Using brads, secure two half circles on the lower edges. Mat photo onto white, black and striped paper. Before mounting photo, use a dry-brush technique, wiping cream paint from the outer edge of the page toward the inside.

Nic Howard, Pukekone,
South Aukland, New Zealand

Supplies: Patterned papers and vellum (KI Memories); rub-on letters (Making Memories); orange, peach, white and black textured cardstocks (Bazzill); black brads; cream acrylic paint; black stamping ink

THE 17 YEAR ITCH

Barb's photos steal the show with the close-up of an actual cicada and the reactions of the kids. Layer and adhere coordinating pieces of torn patterned paper and patterned vellum onto olive green cardstock background; secure papers with brads. Triple mat a variety of cropped photos on cardstock and patterned paper. Print journaling and title on cream vellum and tear edges; adhere with brads. Embellish with charm, tag and ribbon to complete page.

Barb Hogan, Cincinnati, Ohio

Supplies: Patterned papers (Autumn Leaves, Paper Adventures); patterned vellum (Paper Adventures); metal-rimmed tag (Stampin' Up!); clock charm (Card Connection); red grosgrain ribbon (Midori); deep red, evergreen and cream cardstocks; pink vellum; gold brads; stamping inks

the 17 Year ITCH

Periodic Cicadas: Cicadas are flying, plant-sucking insects of the Order Hemiptera. Adult cicadas tend to be large, with prominent wide-set eyes, short antennae, and clear wings held roof-like over the abdomen. Cicadas are probably best known for their conspicuous "songs", which the males make using specialized structures called tymbals, found on the abdomen. Cicadas in a periodical population are synchronized, so that almost all of them mature into adults, mate, and die in the same year. The fact that periodical cicadas remain locked together in time is made even more amazing by their extremely long life-cycles of 13 or 17 years. The 17 year cicadas rose from the ground in 2004 here in Cincinnati to do their famous "Meet and Greet". With twelve BILLION cicadas in town, they were everywhere for about six full weeks.

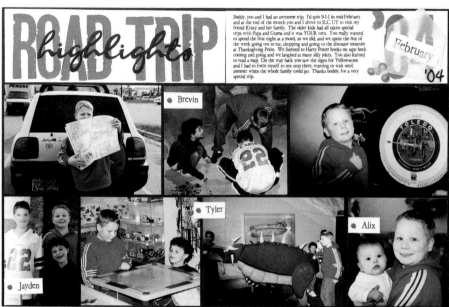

ROAD TRIP HIGHLIGHTS

Cori created two rows of photos which enabled her to tell the whole story of a road trip with her youngest son while using every space on the small spread. Crop each photo and adhere to black cardstock background. Stamp title using red acrylic paint onto white cardstock and add handcut word. Print journaling onto white carstock, trim and stamp year with red acrylic paint. Embellish journaling block with vellum envelope, date and stickers. Print names on white cardstock, trim and adhere to page with small red brads.

Cori Dahmen, Vancouver, Washington

Supplies: Foam letter stamps (Making Memories); die-cut numbers (QuicKutz); M&M's stickers (EK Success); white and black cardstocks; red brads; vellum envelope; red acrylic paint

KEEP ON SEARCHING

Graphic patterned papers in cool ocean colors highlight the curious nature of Annalisa's son as he explored the coast in search of sea lions. Print title on vellum and adhere to patterned paper background using eyelets in each corner. Tie ribbon through eyelets. Mat photos on blue and green cardstocks, mount matted photos onto patterned paper and adhere to the page. Add letter stickers and acrylic words to enhance the focal-point photo. Stamp date onto background.

Annalisa D'Andrea, Menlo Park, California

Supplies: Patterned papers and acrylic words (KI Memories); green ribbon (Li'l Davis Designs); date stamp (Making Memories); letter stickers (American Crafts); violet and chartreuse cardstocks; green eyelets; blue vellum; black stamping ink

TIME

Connie's collaged page gives the illusion of depth by placing some elements underneath a preprinted transparency and others on top. Layer background photos, epoxy stickers, quote sticker and black mesh on speckled cardstock background. Stamp title word several times onto patterned paper using black and light green acrylic paints. Tear words out and add to layout, reserving one. Using spray adhesive, mount transparency onto page. Mat focal-point photo and add at an angle near center. Paint mini frame with black and dry brush with blue. Add photos. Layer frame over reserved word block. Embellish with final quote tag, clock charm and ribbon.

Connie Abbott, Minneapolis, Minnesota

Supplies: *Patterned papers (Club Scrap); vellum quote stickers (Cloud 9 Design); foam letter stamps (Making Memories); word epoxy sticker (Creative Imaginations); transparency (K & Company); spray adhesive (3M); mini frame (PSX Design); watch face charm (7 Gypsies); black cardstock; vellum; mesh; black and light green acrylic paints*

ATLANTA ZOO

Primary colors and basic shapes provide Danielle's page with striking elements that contrast with the neutral background. Adhere patterned paper with animal definitions to background. Use a platter to trace a large half circle onto blue and alphabet cardstocks. Cut out and adhere to right side of page. Modify focal-point photo in image-editing software by adding animal images and title letters. Print and mat onto green cardstock, leaving room on the left side for clips and handwritten journaling. Add butterflies to page. Crop photos and matting using circle cutter. Mount on left side. Embellish page with ribbons and silk flower.

Danielle Thompson, Tucker, Georgia

Supplies: *Patterned papers (Doodlebug Design, Li'l Davis Designs); circle cutting system (Creative Memories); letter stickers (Mrs. Grossman's); butterfly clip art (Dover Publications); ribbons (Offray); black clips (7 Gypsies); silk flower (Prima); green, blue and yellow cardstocks; large corner rounder; staples; blue and black pens; foam adhesive*

WISHES

Shades of pink and green bring bright appeal to Jeniece's page of dandelion wishes. Trim patterned papers horizontally and mount onto green cardstock background. Mat photo on green cardstock and add to page. Adhere laser-cut letters to craft mesh, and weave green yarn around edge of mesh. Cut and adhere a block of striped paper to fit under mesh, making sure the stripes run vertically, and mount title block onto page. Print journaling on clear vellum and adhere over laser-cut block. Cut additional striped paper to fit under journaling block with stripes running vertically. Adhere to page. Trim a number of flowers from paper and mount using foam adhesive. Create bottom border by alternating flowers and miniature framed photos. Apply remaining flowers and add rhinestones.

Jeniece Higgins, Lake Forest, Illinois

Supplies: *Patterned papers (Doodlebug Design, Kangaroo & Joey); leather flowers (Making Memories); wood flowers and frames (Li'l Davis Designs); fibers (Fibers By The Yard); vellum (Paper Company); laser die cuts (source unknown); pink rhinestones; plastic craft mesh; green cardstock; foam adhesives*

EXPLORE DISCOVER

Using word-processing software, Monica created a wave for her journaling and made an initial capital letter from the name of the river her family was visiting. Edge yellow cardstock background with black ink. Trim embossed patterned paper into blocks making sure to include child's initials. Lightly outline the letters, ink edges and finish laying down a color-blocked pattern. Adhere large photo and attach photo corners. Mount small photo onto blue cardstock and ink edges. Create a wave pattern in word-processing software and type journaling. Design a circular element for an initial letter and combine with journaling. Print on blue cardstock and ink edges. Embellish page with words cut from embossed paper and curled wire used to hang a charm.

Monica Kornfeld, Fairbanks, Alaska

Supplies: *Word-processing software (Microsoft Word); embossed paper (K & Company); black photo corners (Canson); jump rings (Making Memories); blue and yellow cardstocks; black craft wire; fishing swivel; heart charm; black stamping ink; black pen*

GRANDMA KEE'S LITTLE BOOK

Melissa altered a child's board book to create a mini album containing photos of a trip to the beach along with witty correspondence from her mother. Sand shiny finish off pages and cover. Paint book with gesso. Using acrylic paint, add color to pages as desired. Adhere ribbon for a tie closure to front and back covers. Print book title onto patterned paper and trim. Add touches of pink acrylic paint and adhere around spine to cover front and back. Add patterned papers to all left pages. Import e-mails into scrapbooking software, resize, print and adhere them over patterned papers. Add photo corners, die cuts and other embellishments to e-mail pages. Crop photos and add to right-hand pages. Embellish with hand-painted brads. Journal names and locations directly onto photos. Embellish cover with buttons, ribbons and charms.

Melissa Smith, North Richland Hills, Texas

Supplies: *Papers and die cuts (Anna Griffin); Creative Scrapbooking Assistant software (Hewlett-Packard); photo corners (Canson); beads; ribbon; buttons; brads; gesso; blue, green and pink acrylic paints; child's board book; sandpaper*

CREATE

Kathryn chose bright and playful colors with a few striking elements to showcase her budding artist. Trim dot and stripes papers and add to pink cardstock background. Print journaling onto a transparency and mount onto striped paper. Print playful words and apply with square conchos. Paint colored conchos with white acrylic paint. Add a gold paper strip across the intersection of the papers and transparency. Embellish with two small circular conchos. Add matted photos. Stamp title onto transparency using turquoise paint. To fill initial and date conchos, trim paper, add rub-on letters and affix over pink patterned paper.

Kathryn Allen, Hamilton, Ohio

Supplies: *Patterned papers (Carolee's Creations, Scrapworks); square and small circle conchos (Scrapworks); foam letter stamps (Making Memories); rub-on letters (Autumn Leaves); word stamps (EK Success); black stamping ink; pink and turquoise cardstocks; transparency; turquoise and white acrylic paints*

A HAT FOR MIMI

Melissa's page showcases her daughter embellishing a crocheted hat and the results that Mimi, the doll, proudly wears. Print journaling onto transparency and adhere. Silhouette cut two large corners of collage paper, edge with black stamping ink and apply. Crop photos and mats. Distress the edges using black ink. Print photo onto canvas paper, mat onto cardstock and ink the mat's edges. Using black ink, impress the ornamental design and letter stamps onto cotton fabric. Add photos and fabric to layout. Embellish page with flowers and brads.

Melissa Smith, North Richland Hills, Texas

Supplies: *Gray and pink collage papers, letter stamps (Rusty Pickle); ornamental stamp (Anna Griffin); corner stamp (Stampin'Up!); printable canvas paper (Vintage Workshop); gray and pink papers; black stamping ink; cotton fabric scraps; copper brads; tassel; silk flowers; transparency*

ALOHA MAHALO

Echoing the projects completed by her sons, Beth created leis by stringing together punched and button flowers. Trim orange patterned paper, mount onto orange cardstock. Dress up a journaling block by impressing a flower stamp onto white paper and printing text over it. Mat it on a torn orange block. Adhere wave-edge strips to bottom of page. Add letter stickers and plastic flowes tied with twine. Adhere sanded photos. Create paper leis by stringing flower buttons and punches. Secure a triangular eyelet on one end of each. Add surfboard stickers to the page and dangle leis.

Beth Ervin, Inver Grove Heights, Minnesota

Supplies: Patterned papers (Cottage Arts, Karen Foster Design, KI Memories); die-cut letters (Sizzix); negative strip, buttons, surfboard and car stickers (Creative Imaginations); flower punch and stamp (Stampin'Up!); vellum; page pebble (Magic Scraps); twine; triangular eyelets (source unknown); decorative scissors (Fiskars); sandpaper; yellow stamping ink; orange and yellow cardstocks

CHRISTMAS CRAFTS

Amy captured her daughter's warm feeling and love for crafts by using vibrant greens and pinks in this design. Trim patterned papers to layer on green cardstock background and ink edges with black ink. Print journaling onto white paper using a bright green background and white letters. Trim journaling into strips, edge with black ink and add to page. Crop photos to the same size and mat together on cardstock. Affix rub-on letters and letter stickers to create title. Outline white letter stickers with black pen. Add epoxy sticker for embellishment.

Amy Stultz, Mooresville, Indiana

Supplies: Patterned papers (KI Memories); rub-on letters (Scrapworks); letter stickers (American Crafts); epoxy sticker (Target); white cardstock; black stamping ink; black pen

SAFARI

Brenda used both patterned and specialty papers to create a safari-style page of her daughter picking strawberries. Layer and adhere patterned papers, mulberry papers and corregated crimped paper onto patterned paper background. Trim two identical blocks of green cardstock. Punch holes in cardstock. Wrap leather cord through holes and tie knot to create fold-out element. Crop and adhere focal-point photo to front of fold-out; embellish with metal accent. Crop two smaller photos for inside. Mat photos onto torn beige cardstock. Add journaling printed on vellum along with metal accent. Wrap and adhere fiber to crimped paper. Place letter stickers along fiber to create title.

Brenda Eastman, Clermont, Florida

Supplies: Patterned papers (Design Originals, DMD); mulberry papers, crimped corregated paper (DMD); title stickers (EK Sucess); fibers and leather cord (Jo-Ann Stores); metal accents (K & Company); vellum

ARTS & CRAFTS

Polly's layout captures her daughter and nephew working on cratfs as he dons a Halloween mask. Create background using monochromatic papers with contrasting patterns. Adhere wider strip on left side. Use die-cut letters for title, saving select negative space scraps. Adhere letters onto four raffle tickets and remaining letters on background. Mat photo onto blue cardstock and orange polka-dot paper. Mat journaling onto black, adding the skull laser cut to the left side. Stamp extra title words, using black ink, onto polka-dot paper strips. Complete stamping on photo mat and metal-rimmed tag. Dress up page with flowers, ribbon and a button.

Polly McMillan, Bullhead City, Arizona

Supplies: Patterned papers (Making Memories); raffle tickets (www.maudeandmillie.com); die-cut letters (QuicKutz); letter stamps (Hero Arts, PSX Design); gingham ribbon (Offray); silk flowers, skull die cut (Wal-Mart); number stickers (Bo-Bunny Press); metal-rimmed tag (Avery); button

IMAGINATION

With a photo of such a bright smile and imaginative personality, Gemiel designed a page with muted papers and a few simple embellishments. Mount strips of paper to top and bottom of page. Add a vellum quote over denim blue strip near the bottom of the page. Print journaling on clear transparency, adhere and add charm. Triple mat photo. Include an extra inch on the bottom edge of the final mat to add ribbon. Adhere to page. Add epoxy stickers.

Gemiel Matthews, Yorktown, Virginia

Supplies: Patterned papers, transparency quote and epoxy stickers (Autumn Leaves); fleur-de-lis charm (source unknown); charm pin (Making Memories); jump rings (Darice); fibers; transparency

KINDERGARTEN PORTRAIT

Aimee provides a fresh look to this page using green gingham paper. Stamp title letters onto background using red paint. Print remainder of title onto transparency, trim and adhere over stamped letters. Embellish with fabric, paper and buttons. Double mat photo onto black and patterned papers. Adhere over a block of notebook paper. Scan schoolwork; reduce image, print and trim. Mount file folder and tuck in schoolwork. Paint a stencil letter and line with patterned paper; adhere to page with black brads. Enrich the design with paper clips, stickers and letter beads on twine.

Aimee Grenier, Hinton, Alberta, Canada
Photos: Jostens, Canada, Edmonton, Alberta, Canada

Supplies: Patterned papers (Deluxe Designs, Mustard Moon); foam letter stamps (Making Memories); school stickers (Pebbles); phrase sticker (source unknown); script sticker (C-Thru Ruler); file folder (Rusty Pickle); stencil letter (Staples); black cardstock; transparency; notebook paper; twine; wood buttons; gingham fabric scraps; black brads; paper clips; red and black pens; letter beads; black stamping ink; red acylic paint

FIRST DAY JITTERS

Layers of sanded elements bring softness to the tender moment in Monica's page. Trim strips from graphic patterned paper, sand and arrange on patterned paper background. To complete the journaling block, print the text onto sanded paper. Add mesh and letter stickers. Print title letters with an added shadow onto transparency and mount over ribbon. Crop photos, sand and gently ink edges and adhere. Add final touches of sewing, labels and date embellishment.

Monica Kornfeld, Fairbanks, Alaska

Supplies: Patterned papers and letter stickers (Basic Grey); label maker (Dymo); polka dot ribbon (Offray); blue mesh (Magic Mesh); black stamping ink; transparency; black pen; sandpaper

K-4

Graphic patterns combine with touches of ribbon and smatterings of ink for Colleen's page about her "baby" going off to school. Mat gingham patterned paper on inked cream cardstock background. Add blocks of inked patterned papers. Print journaling block and mount onto script paper, tying a ribbon around the top. Add letters stickers over ribbon to create title. Adhere additional ribbons near bottom of page, hanging an inked metal-rimmed tag with hand printed date. Mount photos onto page.

Colleen Stearns,
Natrona Heights, Pennsylvania

Supplies: *Patterned papers (Scenic Route Paper Co.); ribbons (Li'l Davis Designs); letter cut-outs (Foofala); distress ink (Ranger); tag (Scrapping with Style); cream cardstock; black pen; brown stamping ink*

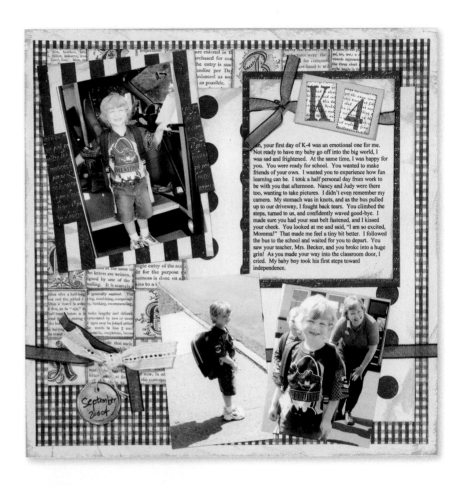

KURTIS

Back-to-school for a new first-grader is a special accomplishment for a 6 year old, and Heather created this funky, chunky page to mark the occasion. Use patterned paper that coordinates with photos to create background. Mat photos onto black cardstock and adhere to page at slight angles. Tear corrugated cardboard and stamp with school phrases and child's name. Adhere to opposite corners of the page. Adhere wooden frame, bottle cap and stickers under the title. Embellish with stickers and a woven label.

Heather Stanworth, Delta, Utah

Supplies: *Patterned papers (7 Gypsies, Pebbles); letter stamps (Leave Memories, Making Memories); yellow "1" sticker (Paper Loft); letter stickers (Chatterbox); raffle ticket stickers, measuring tape number stickers, mini bottle cap, wood frame (Li'l Davis Designs); woven label (Me & My Big Ideas); black cardstock; corrugated cardboard*

WHATEVER YOU ARE

Laurel's page features her daughter sharing her "no fear" attitude as she approaches her kindergarten classroom. For left page, adhere blocks of patterned papers to cardstock background. Trim quote transparency and adhere. Add lace and strip of black cardstock. Mat photos onto cardstock and patterned paper and adhere. Trim patterned paper square and circles; apply rub-on letters and adhere to layout. For right page, adhere blocks of patterned papers to cardstock background. Print journaling on transparency, trim and adhere to layout. Add lace and cardstock trim. Crop photos, mount onto cardstocks and adhere. Trim patterned paper squares and circle, apply rub-on letters and adhere.

Laurel Gervitz, Maple Grove, Minnesota

Supplies: Patterned papers (KI Memories, Li'l Davis Designs); die cuts (KI Memories); rub-on letters (Making Memories); black lace (EK Success); black, pink and brown cardstocks; black and brown stamping inks; transparency

MY LEGACY

Becky's layout shares her feelings of amazement at how fast her children have grown. Cut patterned paper and sherbet-colored cardstock into three blocks and adhere over white cardstock background. Print journaling onto an additional piece of cardstock, trim and adhere. Add photo. Apply white rub-on letters to create title. Secure acrylic charm to metal-rimmed tag with brad and add to page in bottom left corner.

Becky Thompson, Fruitland, Idaho

Supplies: Patterned paper (Rusty Pickle); letter stickers (Creative Imaginations); metal rimmed tag (Avery); acrylic charm (Doodlebug Design); white, pink and peach cardstock; silver brad

Look at those faces - big grins, eyes bright and shiny - just a bundle of excitement, nerves, and sheer joy. Who can look at that and not smile?

The occasion? The first day of school. Adam starts 5th grade, Samantha 6th, and Kristin 2nd. How did my little kids get so big? I can hardly believe my eyes when I look at this picture. It's not the first one I have of the three of you, and it surely won't be the last. But something about it strikes me differently. Maybe it's the fact that I can see the adults you're going to be in just a few short years in your faces. Maybe it's the fact that none of you fit anymore in the crook of my arm the way you did when you were babies. I don't know what it is. Like the way the three of you were feeling on this day, it's a mix of emotions – but most of all, it's just pride. I'm unabashedly, unashamedly proud of the three of you. You are my joy. You are my future. You are my legacy.

My Favorite Subject was

My Best Friends were .

My Favorite Food in the Cafeteria was

Fourth Grade
Mrs. Stetler
1994
It was just another wonderful year at Portola Elementary School. Fourth grade is special for many reasons. In California it is the year of the Mission Project, and we spent hours making a 3-D mission diorama. The highlight of the year was the three day trip to Mesa. The adventure at the Mesa ecology center included camping, hiking, & learning about the natural flora and fauna of Southern California. You also learned how the Chumash Indians lived. Dad shared this wonderful experience with you. You both talked about it for weeks!

GRADE 4

As part of a 21st birthday album, Pamela created this page of her daughter's fourth-grade school year. Layer pink, white and green cardstocks to form a triple mat large enough to hold matted focal-point photo and mini photos along with letter stickers for title. Mount element to patterned paper background. Add copied and mounted "favorites" strips with pink and green brads. Double mat classroom photo and adhere. Print journaling, trim and adhere; add two pink brads for embellishment. Embellish page with die cut squares and pencil. Finish with decorative tag embellished with letter stickers and yellow embroidery floss.

Pamela James, Ventura, California

Supplies: Patterned paper (Bo-Bunny Press); die-cut embellishments (source unknown); letter stickers (source unknown); pencil die cut (Westrim); yellow floss (DMC); hot pink, green and white cardstocks; green and pink brads

4TH GRADER

Renee captured several moments from her daughter's first day of fourth grade. Add a vertical border of brown cardstock to striped patterned paper background. Mat photos with brown and blue cardstocks and adhere. Print journaling, mat and add to the page. Apply epoxy word stickers to blue cardstock, mat and adhere to page. Add ribbon along left edge of brown border and embellish with curly paper clip. Use another piece of ribbon as a photo corner and bow embellishment. Print definition onto white cardstock, mat and adhere over focal-point photo. Apply metal number, round epoxy letter stickers and embossed letters with pink brads to create title. Affix letter stencil over blue cardstock and mat and adhere over focal-point photo.

Renee Foss, Seven Fields, Pennsylvania

Supplies: Patterned paper (SEI); round epoxy letter stickers (EK Success); epoxy word stickers (Creative Imaginations); metal number, curly paper clips, definition sticker, eyelet letters, acrylic paints and magnetic date stamp (Making Memories); letter stencil (Autumn Leaves); blue grosgrain ribbon (Offray); watermark ink (Tsukineko); pink embossing powder; brown and blue cardstocks; brown and pink brads

THERE SHE GOES

Tricia created a vibrant design reflective of her daughter's exuberant personality. For left page, layer patterned paper, inked pink and blue cardstocks and patterned vellum over pink patterned paper background. Mat photo onto inked brown cardstock and adhere; embellish with gingham ribbon. Edge butterscotch tags with brown ink, add die-cut letters, small flowers and ribbon and adhere to page. Add large die-cut flowers embellished with acrylic word charms to page. For right page, layer patterned papers and inked cardstocks to pink patterned paper background. Add die-cut letters and flowers, buttons and acrylic word charms. Double mat photo onto inked pink and brown cardstocks and wrap with gingham ribbon. Affix hinges to create fold-out element. Print journaling onto white cardstock, trim and adhere beneath fold-out. Adhere photo and inked flower die cuts embellished with buttons. Stamp words onto white cardstock, trim and adhere to inked blue cardstock and metal-rimmed tag. Add small flower die cuts and brad to tag.

Tricia Rubens, Castle Rock, Colorado

Supplies: *Patterned papers, vellum and acrylic word charms (KI Memories); letter and flower die cuts (QuicKutz); eyelet hinges (Making Memories); pink gingham ribbon (Offray); pink, blue, brown and butterscotch cardstocks; buttons; metal-rimmed tag; silver brad; rust and blue stamping ink*

MIDDLE SCHOOLER

Alecia was inspired to create this page after she noticed that her daughter was no longer a little girl, but a true "tween." Print journaling onto transparency and paint back with cream paint. Once dry, trim transparency into 3-sided frame. Adhere photo to patterned paper background. Add transparency, cardstock cut-outs and letters stickers. Adhere coin holder over small piece of patterned paper, apply number sticker, rub-on letters and handwritten words and add magnifying glass; adhere element to page.

Alecia Grimm, Atlanta, Georgia

Supplies: Patterned papers and school images cut-out sheet (Blue Cardigan Designs); coin holder and magnifying glass (www. ourvintageshop.com); distress ink (Ranger); letter stickers (SEI); transparency (Grafix); yellow acrylic paint; staples

PJ DAY

Emily enhances the excitement in the photos felt by school children on the very popular "PJ Day" by using hot colors in her design. Print journaling onto striped patterned paper and trim. Cut additional blocks of patterned papers and adhere to patterned paper background. Crop and mat photos and adhere to layout. Affix title letters to metal-rimmed tags. Add ribbons, staples and brads and adhere to layout. Embellish patterned paper with a trio of eyelets, ribbons, rickrack and staples.

Emily Burrough, San Diego, California

Supplies: Patterned paper and letter stickers (K & Company); metal-rimmed tags (Making Memories); ribbons (source unknown); staples

SUMMER FARMER

Lisa cleverly used burlap and cork letter stickers to give her layout a rustic feel. For left page, edge cream cardstock background with brown ink. Trim blocks of patterned paper and green cardstock, ink edges and adhere. Double mat photos onto inked cream and purple cardstocks and adhere. Apply cork letter stickers over green cardstock strip to create title. Using mini safety pins, layer title photo on purple cardstock and burlap square and adhere. Print quote on cream cardstock, ink edges and mat onto green cardstock. Embellish page with small gingham ribbons, gold brads and acrylic letter. For right page, edge cream cardstock background with brown ink and adhere block of patterned paper. Triple mat photos onto cream, purple and green cardstocks with inked edges. Print journaling onto cream cardstock, ink edges and mat onto green cardstock. Embellish page with small burlap square, mini safety pin, gingham ribbons and gold brads.

Lisa Turley, Chesapeake, Virginia

Supplies: Patterned paper (Chatterbox); cork letter stickers (Creative Imaginations); clay phrase (Li'l Davis Designs); green gingham ribbon (Offray); mini safety pins (Making Memories); cream, olive and purple cardstocks; gold brads; burlap scraps; brown stamping ink

FIRST BANK ACCOUNT

LeAnne's layout proves the value of recording hidden treasures. Using image-editing software, crop photos, place them side by side and print as one element. Adhere to top of blue cardstock background. Print journaling onto white cardstock, trim and ink edges with green ink. To make stamps for title, print title letters reversed, directly onto thin craft foam sheet. Cut out letters and apply sticker backing. Adhere to a square of thick tagboard. Add another layer to letter if stamp is not deep enough. Paint letters with acrylic paint and use to stamp on cardstock. Stamp the remainder of title on background.

LeAnne Fritts, Denver, North Carolina

Supplies: Letter stamps (EK Success); alphabet foam stamps (artist's own); green chalk ink (Stampin'Up!); image-editing software (Adobe Photoshop Elements 2.0); black pen; blue cardstock; craft foam; white acrylic paint

When I got this picture back from the developer I was thrilled. At 8 TIM is notorious for wonky and cheesy grins. This one shows a sincere, heart felt smile. We were visiting Auntie in Bothell, WA and the kids went out on the back patio. Just past the grassy area was a huge blackberry patch and even though Tim doesn't care for the taste of the berries he was too happy to pick a bunch for smoothies. One of the things I love about Tim is his ability to take joy in the most basic activities. The other kids are big on being entertained and doing exciting things. Sure, he enjoys those type of activities too, but he doesn't require them to be happy. He never, ever tells us he is bored or that there is nothing to do. He loves playing outside with all the kids in the neighborhood, but he is often found in his special spot, watching a movie, TV or playing with toys. That's my square pants.

BERRY PROUD

Cori should be "berry proud" of her handmade raspberries comprised of inked, punched and layered circles. Print journaling onto tan cardstock and adhere next to large photo on blue cardstock background. Trim two brown strips of cardstock, dry brush with white paint and adhere. Using a zigzag stitch, sew elements to page. Add gingham ribbon. Apply raspberry ink to a sheet of cardstock. Use die-cut letters to create title and year. From the same sheet, punch circles using circle punch; layer circles with foam adhesive and add leaves and wire to mimic raspberries. Add wooden letters to journaling and title.

Cori Dahmen, Vancouver, Washington

Supplies: Wooden letters and tan gingham ribbon (Li'l Davis Designs); die-cut letters (QuicKutz); circle punch (EK Success); silk leaves; blue, brown, tan and white cardstocks; white and red stamping inks

TJ TIES HIS SHOES

Gemiel showcases her son's accomplishment in her layout by using a large photo and simple accents, including a set of eyelets laced with the shoestring from TJ's shoes. Tear patterned vellum and adhere to white cardstock background. Mount focal-point photo, add photo turns and secure with brads. Trim two sections of gray cardstock; add eyelets and lace with a shoestring, tying a bow at one end. Print journaling on white cardstock, adhere over gray cardstock and mount element to page. Add word stickers to a metal frame and mount over photo; add screw-top eyelets.

Gemiel Matthews, Yorktown, Virginia

Supplies: Embossed cardstock, newsprint vellum, word stickers (Club Scrap); metal frame, screw-top eyelets and photo turns (Making Memories); white and gray cardstock; shoe lace; black brads; gray eyelets

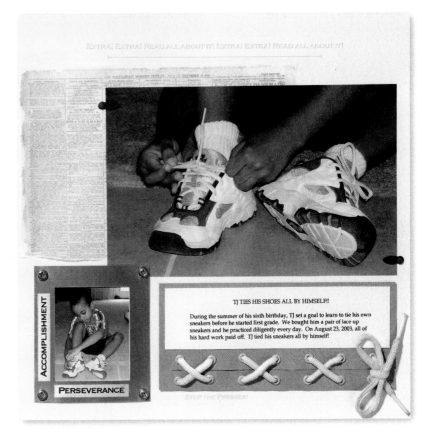

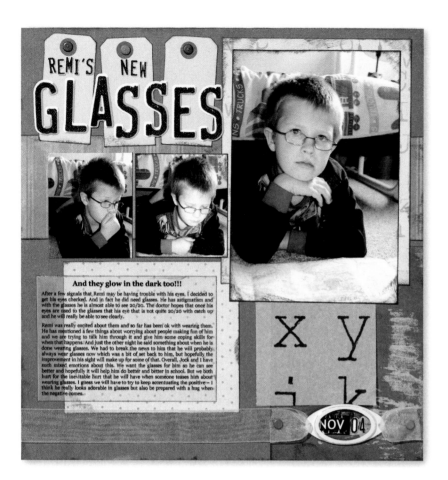

REMI'S NEW GLASSES

Syalynne's pictures capture her son's apprehensive feelings about his new glasses. Ink edges of patterned paper blocks. Adhere blocks and piece of patterned vellum to red cardstock background. Trim cream cardstock and snip upper corners to create a trio of tags. Add a small circle and flathead eyelet to each, ink edges and adhere. Affix title letter stickers. Crop photos, ink edges and adhere. Print journaling onto vellum, trim, ink edges and adhere. String organza ribbon through a round label holder. Add flathead eyelets to anchor ribbon and adhere ribbon ends to back of layout. Affix stickers inside label holder to create date.

Syalynne Kramer,
Colorado Springs, Colorado

Supplies: *Patterned papers (7 Gypsies); letter stickers (Sticker Studio); label holder (Making Memories); organza ribbon; rust and cream cardstocks; flathead eyelets; vellum; medium and dark brown stamping inks*

ALMOST SIX

Simple blocks of color enhance the expressive photo of Kelli's son. Print journaling and portion of title onto block of patterned cardstock, trim and adhere to black cardstock background. Mat photo onto black cardstock and adhere to page. Use a black pen to handwrite remainder of title. Affix number sticker to small red cardstock square and mount onto white cardstock; adhere to page. Stamp date in lower right corner.

Kelli Lawlor, Norfolk, Virginia

Supplies: *Patterned paper (SEI); date stamp (Making Memories); number sticker (Doodlebug Design); black, red and white cardstock; black stamping ink; black pen*

ALL AT ONCE!

Tricia cleverly utilized an old pair of blue jeans as a mat for her focal-point photo. For left page, print title onto transparency and trim. Mat focal-point photo onto piece of blue jeans material. Whitewash patterned paper block to tone down color and tear. Layer patterned paper, red mesh, silver mesh, wire, border sticker, transparency and photo onto patterned paper background. Embellish page with twine, denim ties, lock, keys, button eyelets and screw-top eyelets. For right page, print title and journaling onto transparency and trim. Layer transparency, red mesh, silver mesh, patterned paper, photos and denim scrap onto patterned paper background. Embellish vellum with star brads, twine and denim ties.

Tricia Rubens, Castle Rock, Colorado

Supplies: Patterned papers (Rusty Pickle); red and silver mesh (Magic Mesh); word rivet brads and star brads (Creative Impressions); duct tape patterned paper (Pebbles); faux button hole belt sticker (Sweetwater); screw-top eyelets (Making Memories); luggage lock and keys (7 Gypsies); denim fabric or blue jeans material; star brads; copper wire; twine; transparency

CATALINA'S NEW SMILE

Michaela documented the excitement of her daughter's lost tooth by using before and after pictures. Trim strips of red and green cardstocks, ink edges and adhere to blue cardstock background. Print first block of journaling onto green cardstock, trim into circle and ink edges. Print second block of journaling onto transparency and trim into vertical strip. Crop photos and mount onto inked red cardstock. Layer cardstocks, journaling and photos onto background. Add rub-on letters and letter stickers to create title. Apply rub-on letters to square brads and add to photo mats.

Michaela Young-Mitchell, Morenci, Arizona

Supplies: Black rub-on letters (Making Memories); transparency, square and tooth letter stickers (Karen Foster Design); blue, bright green and raspberry cardstocks (Bazzill); square brads; black stamping ink

DAY, YEARS, LIFETIME

Sande created a journaling pocket by machine stitching blocks of patterned cardstock. For left page, trim blocks of patterned cardstock and machine stitch over black cardstock background leaving one section open to create pocket. Using image-editing software, add white journaling to focal-point photo, mount onto red cardstock and embellish with patterned paper and brads. Use wooden letters and rub-on letters applied to cardstocks to create title. Print journaling and photos onto white cardstock and trim into blocks. Mount first block onto red cardstock; punch hole in all blocks and bind together with ribbon. Add metal-rimmed tag, red cardstock stencil matted on patterned paper and charms to embellish. For right page, print quote onto red cardstock, trim and apply rub-on letters. Trim additional blocks of patterned cardstock and machine stitch to black cardstock background. Mat cropped photos onto patterned cardstock, trim, punch holes and adhere. Embellish with gingham ribbon and silver brads.

Sande Krieger, Salt Lake City, Utah

Supplies: Patterned papers (7 Gypsies); wood letters (Li'l Davis Designs); ribbons (May Arts); metal rimmed tags (Office Max); music note charm (Frost Creek Charms); frame charm (K & Company); number stencil (Home Depot); rub-on letters (Creative Imaginations); red, white and black cardstocks; silver brads

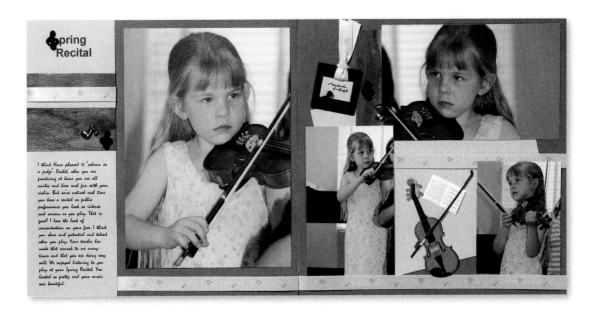

Spring Recital

Using monochromatic hues with touches of delicate ribbon, Ginger created a sweet, feminine spread of her daughter's recital. For left page, print title and journaling on powder blue cardstock, trim, add veneer paper, ribbons and charms. Adhere element along with cropped photo to blue cardstock background. Add an additional ribbon at bottom for embellishment. For right page, trim blocks of powder blue cardstock and veneer paper. Layer along with cropped photos onto blue cardstock background. Add ribbons, black slide mount, charms and violin die cuts.

Ginger McSwain, Cary, North Carolina

Supplies: *Wood veneer (Club Scrap); music note buttons (Jesse James); ribbon (Offray); violin with music embellishments (EK Success); black slide mount (Magic Scraps); blue and powder blue cardstocks; black pen*

Love My Trumpet

Vibrant pinks with hints of blue show off Polly's photos of her daughter playing the trumpet. Mat red dot paper onto turquoise cardstock. Stamp journaling onto striped paper and trim into strips. Crop two more strips of striped paper and adhere. Circle punch turquoise paper and crop a photo. Crop other photos and mount onto page. Die cut photo corners and title letters. Add to page. Tie several lengths of ribbon together to create a top border and add letter buttons. Place brads in acrylic labels and mount together on blue circle. Apply sticker letters on top.

Polly McMillan, Bullhead City, Arizona

Supplies: *Patterned papers, acrylic letters and tiles (Junkitz); die-cut letters, die-cut photo corners (QuicKutz); ribbons (Offray); letter stickers (Creative Imaginations); circle punch (EK Success); letter stamps (PSX Design); pink and white brads; black stamping ink; turquoise cardstock*

RED, WHITE & BLUE

Carrying the colors at a Pack meeting is a proud moment for any scout, and Renee used patriotic colors on her layout to match this theme. Stamp title at bottom of patterned paper background. Crop photos, mount onto torn blue cardstock and adhere to background. Weave ribbon through rectangular holes. Add dimensional stickers mounted with backing paper. Add button embellishments and handwrite date on sticker frame.

Renee Foss, Seven Fields, Pennsylvania

Supplies: *Patterned paper (Daisy D's); striped ribbon (May Arts); patriotic stickers and buttons (K & Company); letter stamps (Stampin' Up!); distress ink (Ranger); double hole ribbon punch (McGill); blue cardstock; black pen*

BLUE AND GOLD

Using color-blocking templates, Christa created this page quickly and creatively. Lay template over blue cardstock background. Lightly trace openings of template with a pencil. Choose elements for each space and crop if needed. Embellish elements with matting, handwritten journaling, ribbons, letter stickers and stamps. Using pencil lines as a guide, adhere elements to the page.

Christa Hamilton, Pearland, Texas

Supplies: *Layout template (Deluxe Designs); Fleur-de-lis paper (It Takes Two); letter stamps, letter stickers and circle punch (EK Success); organza ribbon (Offray); gold floss (DMC); label maker (Dymo); blue and gold cardstock; blue stamping ink; blue pen*

DAISY SCOUTS

Blocks of contrasting colors bring out the bright clothes in Cori's photos. Sew strips of patterned paper and red cardstock onto green cardstock background. Mat one photo with green cardstock; adhere along with additional photos to page. Affix title stickers onto strips of inked red cardstock; embellish with polka-dot ribbon and black brads. Print journaling onto white cardstock, trim, ink edges and adhere. Affix number stickers onto journaling block and secure green metal frame with black brads over date.

Cori Dahmen, Vancouver, Washington

Supplies: *Word patterned paper (Carolee's Creations); letter stickers (Doodlebug Design); ribbon (May Arts); green metal frame (Making Memories); number stickers (Boxer Scrapbook Productions, Colorbök, Doodlebug Design, Me & My Big Ideas); green, evergreen and raspberry cardstock; black brads; black stamping ink*

GIRL SCOUTS

Holly shows the sweet and feminine side of scouting on this page. Trim large block of olive green cardstock and mount onto purple cardstock background. Trim circle from polka-dot patterned paper and machine stitch onto background. Handcut a purple heart, sew a zigzag stitch around edges and adhere over polka-dot circle. Print journaling onto white cardstock, trim and ink edges. Layer journaling and cropped photos to background. Handcut title and edge with black ink. Add binding, embellished with rub-on letters, ribbons, flowers and brads. Trim photo to fit into metal-rimmed tag, embellish with ribbon and flower and adhere to page.

Holly Corbett, Central, South Carolina

Supplies: *Polka-dot paper (Chatterbox); metal-rimmed tag, black rub-on letters (Making Memories); tri-colored grosgrain ribbon (Li'l Davis Designs); gingham binding tape (Wrights); paper flowers (Michaels); white photo corners (Pioneer); olive, purple and white cardstocks; black brads; decorative-edge scissors; black stamping ink*

At a loss for a too-perfect-for-words page title? Remedy your "writer's block" by utilizing the lists of sample sentiments below for creative inspiration. You can custom-coordinate your page titles with handmade or computer-generated design. For additional artistic flair, accent page titles with embellishments that speak to your pictures and provide added punch to your page theme.

LIVE

100% Kid
Been There, Done That
Birthday Bashes
Birthday Wishes
Born to Play
Bubbles Galore
Catch That Kid
Crayon Creations
Dance Like No One's Watching
Dare to Dream
Dressin' Up
Fantasy Fun
Finding the Fun Factor
Full of Life
Fun & Games
Going Places
Hangin' at the Playground
Homemade Fun
Hunting for Anything
Just Singin' in the Rain
Kid Power
Let It Snow, Let It Snow
Let's Go Fly a Kite
Lights! Camera! Action!
Live It Up!
Make a Wish
New Experiences, New Adventures
Oh, the Places You'll Go
One of a Kind
Our Skate Date
Pumpkin Patch
Put on Your Dancin' Shoes
Quest for Fun
Rainy Day Fun
Ready, Set, Go
Ridin' Waves
Rockin' and Splashin'

Smell Those Cookies!
Snowday
Splish Splash
Summer Fun
Takin' It Easy
We've Got Tickets to Ride
Wet and Wild at the Water Park
What Childhood Is All About
X Marks the Spot

LOVE

Always Be You
Crazy Little Thing Called Love
Daddy Love
Demonstrating Joy
Expressions of Love
Finding Joy
Guess How Much
I Love You?
Hugs and Kisses
I Love You
In Your Eyes
Joyful Heart
Just Because I Love You
Just Because You're Special
Love at First Sight
Love Defined
Love You Always
Love You Forever
Loving You
Mommy Love
My Greatest Love
A Place to Dream
My Precious One
Reflections of You
Things I Love About You
Today You Are You

Who Do I Love?
You Are My Shining Star
You Are My Sunshine
You Melt My Heart
You'll Be in My Heart

LAUGH

All About You
All Smiles
Beaming With Joy
Burst of Laughter
Chuckles
Crackin' Up
Crazy You
Emotions Run Wild
Expressions of Joy
Free Spirit
Funny Faces
Giddy Kids
Gigglebox
Giggles
Glee
Great Big Grin
Happy Faces
Laugh Out Loud
Laughing Eyes
Laughter
Merry Little Tykes
Silly
A Smile Can Happen
Smiley Face
Smiley Punks
A Spoonful of Sugar
What a Riot
Witty Sentiments
You Got Me in Stitches
You Make Me Smile

LEARN

All the World's a Stage
Born Reader
Collecting Bugs and Butterflies
Continuing Traditions
Crazy Olympics
Creativity Counts
Curious Kid
Dare to Explore
Days, Years, Lifetime
First-Day Jitters
First Day of School
The Great Outdoors
Head of the Class
Hit the Books
Imagination
Keep on Searching
Mommy's Little Helper
Musical Magic
My Little Bookworm
Nature All Around
Nature Kid
Open the Treasure Chest
Puzzlemania
Saving Souvenirs
School Bells
The Sky's the Limit
Unexpected Treasures
Watch Out World
Wheels on the Bus
You're an All-Star

ADDITIONAL CREDITS AND INSTRUCTIONS

Cover

Tear along top and bottom edge of dictionary page. Mount on green cardstock and highlight definition with yellow vellum. Mount photo on blue cardstock and tear bottom edge. Stamp title on a small piece of yellow cardstock and adhere to layout. Place metal frame over title and wrap both ends with ribbon. Adhere loose ends of ribbon to layout. Accent with smiley face and crayon embellishments.

Torrey Scott, Thornton, Colorado
Photo: Allison Orthner, Calgary, Alberta, Canada
Supplies: Metal frame (Making Memories); ribbon (Offray); crayon and smiley face embellishments (source unknown); vellum; blue, green and white cardstocks; black stamping ink

Page 1 Every Child Is a Success Story

Tear along edges of brown cardstock. Lightly ink edges using black ink and affix to light tan cardstock. Adhere tan cardstock on top of brown. Accent sides of tan cardstock with black and white ribbon fastened in each corner with decorative brads. Use rub-on letters to create title, spelling the word "success" with foam stamps and paint. Mat photo with brown and white cardstock, and attach to page.

Suzy West, Fremont, California
Supplies: Cardstock (Bazzill); ribbon (Offray); brads, rub-on letters, stamps, paint (Making Memories)

Page 3 Bookplate

Stamp squares onto a small piece of white cardstock using red, blue and yellow ink, using yellow ink on edges. Affix to front of book with red brads. Attach silver letter slide charms to red ribbon, spelling title. Attach to book using glue dots. Finish by tying various pieces of red, blue and yellow ribbon to spiral binding on book.

Jodi Amidei, Memory Makers Books
Supplies: Book (Club Scrap); ribbon (Me & My Big Ideas, Offray, Stampin' Up!); slide charms (Making Memories); square stamp (Hero Arts); ink; brads; white cardstock

Page 6 Best Buddies

Cut varying sizes of circles from patterned papers. Ink edges. Print journaling and crop into block. Crop photos, round corners and ink edges. Stamp title with gray ink down left side of page. Handcut title and adhere along left edge of photo, over stamped title. Add circles, photos and journaling block. Embellish with metal charms and ribbons.

Jodi Amidei, Memory Makers Books
Photos: Ken Trujillo, Memory Makers
Supplies: Patterned paper (Scenic Route Paper Co.); metal charms (Making Memories, Pebbles); letter stamps (River City Rubber Works); white cardstock; black and gray stamping inks; ribbon

Page 7 Smile

Begin with stitched cardstock background and adhere paint chip and yellow journaling block. Apply rub-on letters beside journaling block. Layer boy transparency on top, placing adhesive only where a page element will cover it. Add ribbon with acrylic slider to focal-point photo. Mount photos and add other acrylic embellishments.

Jodi Amidei, Memory Makers Books
Supplies: Stitched cardstock and acrylic words (Westrim); transparency (Hot Off The Press); tri-colored ribbon (Offray); acrylic heart blocks (Heidi Grace Designs); acrylic ribbon slider (Pebbles); black rub-on letters (Making Memories); blue, red and yellow cardstocks; paint chip

Page 9 Athletically Inclined

Trim bamboo paper and adhere to black cardstock. Mat metal border and add to left side of page. Crop, mat and adhere focal-point photo. Print title letters, trim and cover with liquid lacquer. Print, mat and adhere journaling block. Print three photos together and cover with transparency. Tie twine around left side and attach hinges on right. Add a matted photo to the right side of hinges. To cover journaling block, use super sticky adhesive dots to adhere the single photo, while allowing the negative strip to swing side to side. Embellish with metal elements and bamboo strip.

Shannon Taylor, Bristol, Tennessee
Supplies: Bamboo textured paper (Be Unique); metal border (Anima Designs); dimensional adhesive (JudiKins); negative transparency (Creative Imaginations); ball chain (Magic Scraps); gold bar (7 Gypsies); black cardstock; twine; gold stencil letter; gold brads; mini frame; hinges

Page 33 You Are My Greatest Love

Tear side of patterned paper and adhere to cardstock. Double mount green and yellow cardstock squares and affix to page. Adhere strip of patterned paper to bright green cardstock. Mount photo onto squares on a diagonal. Lay mesh over letter stencil and back with patterned paper. Embellish with brads and photo turns. Print title onto vellum strip and mount onto brown cardstock strip. Adhere across top of photo with left edge under stencil. Embellish with spiral clip. Splatter an index card with ink and ink edges. Print journaling onto index card. Slip behind photo, and secure with brads and photo turns. Print title onto small piece of vellum and mount onto small piece of brown cardstock. Attach to page above stencil. Attach yellow buttons to left side of page. Smudge small rectangle of beige cardstock with brown ink and adhere to lower right corner of page. Embellish with silver diamond brads. Affix smaller photos. Embellish with spiral clip, silk flowers and buttons.

Kimberly Billings, East Troy, Wisconsin
Supplies: Patterned paper (Creative Imaginations); cardstock (Bazzill); photo anchors, yellow silk flower, stitches (Making Memories); yellow buttons (EK Success); ink (7 Gypsies); brads; pink buttons; spiral clip; vellum; date stamp; letter stencil; white silk flower; index card; mesh; brown stamping ink

Page 59 Laugh Out Loud

Triple mat photo onto blue, red, and white cardstock with strip of patterned paper at bottom. Embellish top left corner of blue cardstock mat with red photo corner. Adhere strip of striped paper to bottom of blue cardstock, and mount matted photo on top. Print title onto white cardstock, and cut out with a craft knife. Print journaling onto white cardstock and mount onto red cardstock. Adhere next to photo. Affix title to page. Fold small strips of red and blue cardstock and patterned paper. Adhere to page, and embellish page with white rivets at bottom.

Courtney Walsh, Winnebago, Illinois
Supplies: Patterned paper, cardstock, rivets (Chatterbox)

Page 81 Bookworm

Tear red cardstock to cover slightly more than half the page. Mount photo. Load foam stamps with red acrylic paint and impress onto upper right edge of page, traversing the photo and cardstock. Clean stamps and ink intermittently with yellow paint and stamp over the red letters. Tie wire-edged ribbon around page, placing bow near bottom left corner. Print journaling on cardstock and trim. Mat onto white cardstock and adhere to page. Add leather flower and wood letter. Create journaling book by trimming heavy cardstock. Decoupage torn sections of tissue paper onto cover. Print list of favorite books and add to book center. Attach ribbon tie as the pages go in the book. Adhere book to page.

Tamara Morrison, Trabuco Canyon, California
Supplies: Foam letter stamps, red and yellow acrylic paints, leather flower and red silk ribbon (Making Memories); wood letter (Li'l Davis Designs); red patterned tissue paper (DMD); decoupage medium (Plaid); wire-edged floral ribbon (source unknown); red, white and yellow cardstocks (Bazzill); black chalk ink (Tsukineko); tag board

SOURCE GUIDE

The following companies manufacture products featured in this book. Please check your local retailers to find these materials, or go to a company's Web site for the latest product. In addition, we have made every attempt to properly credit the items mentioned in this book. We apologize to any company that we have listed incorrectly, and we would appreciate hearing from you.

3L Corp.
(800) 828-3130
www.scrapbook-adhesives.com
3M
(800) 364-3577
www.3m.com
7 Gypsies
(800) 588-6707
www.7gypsies.com
A.C. Moore
www.acmoore.com
Adobe
www.adobe.com
Alien Skin Software, LLC
(888) 921-SKIN
www.alienskin.com
All Night Media- see Plaid Enterprises
American Crafts
(801) 2226-0747
www.americancrafts.com
American Tag Company
(800) 223-3956
www.americantag.net
Amscan, Inc.
(800) 444-8887
www.amscan.com
Anima Designs
(800) 570-6847
www.animadesigns.com
Anna Griffin, Inc.
(888) 817-8170
www.annagriffin.com
Arctic Frog
(479) 636-FROG
www.arcticfrog.com
ARTchix Studio
(250) 370-9985
www.artchixstudio.com
Art Impressions
(800) 393-2014
www.artimpressions.com
Artistic Expressions
(219) 764-5158
www.artisticexpressionsinc.com
Autumn Leaves
(800) 588-6707
www.autumnleaves.com
Avery Dennison Corporation
(800) GO-AVERY
www.avery.com
Basic Grey™
(801) 451-6006
www.basicgrey.com
Bazzill Basics Paper
(480) 558-8557
www.bazzillbasics.com
Be Unique
(909) 927-5357
www.beuniqueinc.com
Beadery®, The
(401) 539-2432
www.thebeadery.com
Beads & Plenty More- no contact info
Blue Cardigan Designs
(770) 904-4320
www.bluecardigan.com
Bo-Bunny Press
(801) 771-4010
www.bobunny.com
Boxer Scrapbook Productions
(503) 625-0455
www.boxerscrapbooks.com
Canson®, Inc.
(800) 628-9283
www.canson-us.com
Card Connection- see Michaels

Carolee's Creations®
(435) 563-1100
www.ccpaper.com
Chatterbox, Inc.
(208) 939-9133
www.chatterboxinc.com
Clearsnap, Inc.
(360) 293-6634
www.clearsnap.com
Close To My Heart®
(888) 655-6552
www.closetomyheart.com
Cloud 9 Design
(763) 493-0990
www.cloud9design.biz
Club Scrap™
(888) 634-9100
www.clubscrap.com
Collections- no contact info
Colorbök™, Inc.
(800) 366-4660
www.colorbok.com
Craf-T Products
(507) 235-3996
www.craf-tproducts.com
Crafts, Etc. Ltd.
(800) 888-0321
www.craftsetc.com
Creative Imaginations
(800) 942-6487
www.cigift.com
Creative Impressions Rubber Stamps, Inc.
(719) 596-4860
www.creativeimpressions.com
Creative Memories®
(800) 468-9335
www.creativememories.com
Creative Paperclay Company®
(805) 484-6648
www.paperclay.com
Cropper Hopper™/Advantus Corporation
(800) 826-8806
www.cropperhopper.com
C-Thru® Ruler Company, The
(800) 243-8419
www.cthruruler.com
Current®, Inc.
(800) 848-2848
www.currentinc.com
Daisy D's Paper Company
(888) 601-8955
www.daisydspaper.com
Darby
(469) 223-4308
www.darbypaper.com
Darice, Inc.
(800_ 321-1494
www.darice.com
DecoArt™, Inc.
(800) 367-3047
www.decoart.com
Delta Technical Coatings, Inc.
(800) 423-4135
www.deltacrafts.com
Deluxe Designs
(480) 205-9210
www.deluxedesigns.com
Design Originals
(800) 877-0067
www.d-originals.com
Destination™ Scrapbook Designs
(866) 806-7826
www.destinationstickers.com
DieCuts with a View™
(877) 221-6107
www.dcwv.com
DMC Corp.
(973) 589-0606
www.dmc.com
DMD Industries, Inc.
(800) 805-9890
www.dmdind.com
Doodlebug Design™ Inc.
(801) 966-9952
www.doodlebugdesigninc.com
Dover Publications, Inc.
(800) 223-3130
www.doverpublications.com
Dymo
www.dymo.com
Eco Africa-USA (by Signature Plus, Ltd.)
(330) 896-2343
www.naturallypaper.com
Educational Insights
(800) 995-4436www.edin.com

EK Success™, Ltd.
(800) 524-1349
www.eksuccess.com
Far and Away
(509) 340-0124
www.farandawayscrapbooks.com
Fibers by the Yard™
(405) 364-8066
www.fibersbytheyard.com
Fiskars®, Inc.
(800) 950-0203
www.fiskars.com
Flair® Designs
(888) 546-9990
www.flairdesignsinc.com
FontWerks
www.fontwerks.com
FoofaLa
(402) 758-0863
www.foofala.com
Fredrix Artist Canvas
www.fredrixartistcanvas.com
Frost Creek Charms
(763) 684-0074
www.frostcreekcharms.com
Gartner Studios, Inc.
www.uprint.com
Go West Studios
(214) 227-0007
www.goweststudios.com
Grafix®
(800) 447-2349
www.grafix.com
Graphic Products Corporation
(800) 323-1660
www.gpcpapers.com
Hampton Art Stamps, Inc.
(800) 229-1019
www.hamptonart.com
Happy Hammer, The
(303) 690-3883
www.thehappyhammer.com
Headline- no contact info
Heidi Grace Designs
(866) 89heidi
www.heidigrace.com
Hero Arts® Rubber Stamps, Inc.
(800) 822-4376
www.heroarts.com
Hewlett-Packard Company
www.hp.com/go/scrapbooking
Hirschberg Schutz & Co., Inc.
(800) 221-8640
Home Depot U.S.A., Inc.
www.homedepot.com
Hot Off The Press, Inc.
(800) 227-9595
www.paperpizazz.com
Hunt Corporation
(800) 879-4868
www.hunt-corp.com
Ideal- no contact info
Ilford Imaging USA, Inc.
(888) 727-4751
www.printasiafun.com
Imagination Project, Inc.
(513) 860-2711
www.imaginationproject.com
Impress Rubber Stamps
(206) 901-9101
www.impressrubberstamps.com
Inkadinkado® Rubber Stamps
(800) 888-4652
www.inkadinkado.com
It Takes Two®
(800) 331-9843
www.ittakestwo.com
Jaquard Products/Rupert, Gibbon & Spider, Inc.
(800) 442-0455
www.jacquardproducts.com
Jesse James & Co., Inc.
(610) 435-0201
www.jessejamesbutton.com
Jest Charming
(702) 564-5101
www.jestcharming.com
Jo-Ann Stores
(888) 739-4120
www.joann.com
JudiKins
(310) 515-1115
www.judikins.com
Junkitz™
(732) 792-1108
www.junkitz.com

K & Company
(888) 244-2083
www.kandcompany.com
K & S® Metals
(773) 586-8503
www.ksmetals.com
Karen Foster Design
(801) 451-9779
www.karenfosterdesign.com
Keeping Memories Alive™
(800) 419-4949
www.scrapbooks.com
KI Memories
(972) 243-5595
www.kimemories.com
Kopp Design
(801) 489-6011
www.koppdesign.com
Krylon®
(216) 566-200
www.krylon.com
Lara's Crafts
(800) 232-5272
www.larascrafts.com
Leave Memories
www.leavememories.com
Leaving Prints
(801) 426-0636
www.leavingprints.com
Li'l Davis Designs
(949) 838-0344
www.lildavisdesigns.com
Limited Edition Rubberstamps
(650) 594-4242
www.limitededitionrs.com
Loersch Corporation USA
(610) 264-5641
www.loersch.com
Ma Vinci's Reliquary
http://crafts.dm.net/
mall/reliquary/
Magenta Rubber Stamps
(800) 565-5254
www.magentastyle.com
Magic Mesh
(651) 345-6374
www.magicmesh.com
Magic Scraps
(972) 238-1838
www.magicscraps.com
Making Memories
(800) 286-5263
www.makingmemories.com
Manto Fev™
(402) 505-3752
www.mantofev.com
Marvy® Uchida/ Uchida of America, Corp.
(800) 541-5877
www.uchida.com
Mary Engelbreit Studios
(800) 443-MARY
www.maryengelbreit.com
May Arts
(800) 442-3950
www.mayarts.com
McGill, Inc.
(800) 982-9884
www.mcgillinc.com
me & my BiG ideas®
(949) 883-2065
www.meandmybigideas.com
Melissa Frances/Heart & Home, Inc.
(905) 686-9031
www.melissafrances.com
Memories Complete™, LLC
(866) 966-6365
www.memoriescomplete.com
Memories in the Making/Leisure Arts
(800) 643-8030
www.leisurearts.com
Memory Lane- no contact info
Michaels® Arts & Crafts
(800) 642-4235
www.michaels.com
Microsoft Corporation
www.microsoft.com
Midori
(800) 659-3049
www.midoriribbon.com
MOD-my own design
(303) 641-8680
www.mod-myowndesign.com
Morex Corporation
(717) 852-7771
www.morexcorp.com

Mrs. Grossman's Paper Company
(800) 429-4549
www.mrsgrossmans.com
Mustard Moon™
(408) 299-8542
www.mustardmoon.com
My Mind's Eye™, Inc.
(801) 298-3709
www.frame-ups.com
National Cardstock- no longer in business
NRN Designs
(800) 421-6958
www.nrndesigns.com
Nunn Design
(360) 379-3557
www.nunndesign.com
Office Max
www.officemax.com
Office Works
www.officeworks.com.au
Offray
www.offray.com
On Ths Surface
(847) 675-2520
Paper Adventures®
(800) 727-0699
www.paperadventures.com
Paper Co., The/ANW Crestwood
(800) 525-3196
www.anwcrestwood.com
PaperCraft Australia/SSS Pty. Ltd.
www.sewingcraft.com
Paper Fever, Inc.
(800) 477-0902
www.paperfever.com
Paper House Productions®
(800) 255-7316
www.paperhouseproductions.com
Paper Loft
(801) 446-7249
www.paperloft.com
Paper Palette LLC, The
(801) 849-8338
www.stickybackpaper.com
Paper Studio, The- no contact info
Pebbles Inc.
(801) 224-1857
www.pebblesinc.com
Penny Black Rubber Stamps, Inc.
(510) 849-1883
www.pennyblackinc.com
Pioneer Photo Albums, Inc.®
(800) 366-3686
www.pioneerphotoalbums.com
Pixie Press
(888) 834-2883
www.pixiepress.com
Plaid Enterprises, Inc.
(800) 842-4197
www.plaidonline.com
Prima
(909) 627-5532
www.mulberrypaperflowers.com
Prism™
(866) 902-1002
www.prismpapers.com
Provo Craft®
(888) 577-3545
www.provocraft.com
Prym-Dritz Corporation
www.dritz.com
PSX Design™
(800) 782-6748
www.psxdesign.com
Purple Onion Designs
www.purpleoniondesigns.com
QuicKutz
(801) 765-1144
www.quickutz.com
Ranger Industries, Inc.
(800) 244-2211
www.rangerink.com
Rebekka Erickson- see PaperCraft Australia/SSS Pty. Ltd.
Remember When- no contact info
Reminders of Faith™
(724) 827-8549
www.remindersoffaith.com
River City Rubber Works
(877) 735-2276
www.rivercityrubberworks.com
Rusty Pickle
(801) 272-2280
www.rustypickle.com

Scenic Route Paper Co.
(801) 785-0761
www.scenicroutepaper.com
ScrapGoods™ (a division of The Scrap Pack)
www.scrapgoods.com
Scrapping With Style
(704) 254-6238
www.scrappingwithstyle.com
Scrappy Cat™, LLC
(440) 234-4850
www.scrappycatcreations.com
Scrapworks, LLC
(801) 363-1010
www.scrapworks.com
SEI, Inc.
(800) 333-3279
www.shopsei.com
Sizzix®
(866) 742-4447
www.sizzix.com
Sonburn, Inc.
(800) 527-7505
www.sonburn.com
S.R.M. Press, Inc.
(800) 323-9589
www.srmpress.com
Staedtler®, Inc.
(800) 927-7723
www.staedtler.us
Stamp Craft- see Plaid Enterprises
Stampin' Up!®
(800) 782-6787
www.stampinup.com
Stampington & Company
(877) STAMPER
www.stampington.com
Staples, Inc.
(800) 3STAPLE
www.staples.com
Sticker Studio™
(208) 322-2465
www.stickerstudio.com
Stockwell- no contact info
Sugarloaf Products, Inc.
(770) 484-0722
www.sugarloafproducts.com
Suze Weinberg Design Studio
(732) 761-2400
www.schmoozewithsuze.com
Sweetwater
(800) 359-3094
www.sweetwaterscrapbook.com
Target
www.target.com
Textured Trio- no contact info
Trim-Tex, Inc.
(800) 874-2333
www.trim-tex.com
Trodat® GmBH
www.trodat.net
Tsukineko®, Inc.
(800) 769-6633
www.tsukineko.com
Tumblebeasts LLC
(505) 323-5554
www.tumblebeasts.com
vintage workshop™ LLC, the
(913) 341-5559
www.thevintageworkshop.com
Wal-Mart Stores, Inc.
(800) WALMART
www.walmart.com
Westrim® Crafts
(800) 727-2727
www.westrimcrafts.com
Willow Bead
(866) 488-2323
www.willowbead.com
Wordsworth
(719) 282-3495
www.wordsworthstamps.com
WorldWin Paper
(888) 843-6455
www.thepapermill.com
Wrights® Ribbon Accents
(877) 597-4448
www.wrights.com
Yasutomo and Company
(650) 737-8888
www.yasutomo.com
Z-International- no contact info

INDEX